Companion Planting for Beginners

Practical Guide to Organic Gardening. How to Reduce Pests and Fight Disease Without Chemicals. Crop Rotation can be Used to Boost Yield.

© Copyright 2023 by Kevin S. Stevenson

Kevin S. Stevenson
Companion Planting for Beginners

© Copyright 2023 by Kevin S. Stevenson - **All rights reserved**.

This book contains material protected by international and federal copyright laws and treaties. Any reprinting or unauthorized use of this material is prohibited. No part of this book may be reproduced or transmitted in any form or by any means, electronic or mechanical, including photocopying, recording, or by any information storage and retrieval system without the express written permission of the author.

Disclaimer

The information contained in this book is for general information purposes only.

Although we strive to keep the information up to date and correct, we make no representations or warranties of any kind, express or implied, about the completeness, accuracy, reliability, suitability or availability with respect to the book or the information, products, services or related graphics contained in the book for any purpose. Any reliance on such information is therefore strictly at your own risk.

None of the information contained in this book should be interpreted as medical advice. Always consult a medical profession before making any dietary changes in your life.

The author of this book is not a professional specialized in food safety or any other related field. Neither the author nor the publisher is liable for any damages resulting from the use or misuse of the information provided in this book.

Kevin S. Stevenson
Companion Planting for Beginners

Table of Contents

CHAPTER 1 - What is Companion Planting? 7

CHAPTER 2 - How to realize the Garden 9

    Sun vs Partial Shadow 11

CHAPTER 3 – Companion Planting Benefits 15

    How do you identify the companion plants? 17

CHAPTER 4 - What are the plants to associate in the garden? 19

CHAPTER 5 - The Herbal Association 21

CHAPTER 6 - Organic gardening and Companion Planting 25

CHAPTER 7 - Allelopathy 27

CHAPTER 8 - Insects 29

    Good and Bad 29

CHAPTER 9 - Beneficial Insects in the Garden 33

    What useful insects are and how they work? 33
    Useful insects for gardens and vegetable gardens 35
        Ladybugs 36
        Osmia 41
        Nematode 42
        Praying Mantis 45
        Pollinating insects 46
        Mealybugs 51
        Green Lacewings 58
        Damsel Bugs 59
        Parasitic Wasps 61
        Spiders 63
        Predator flies 64
    Common insect pests 67
        Aphids 67

- Asparagus Beetles 71
- Cabbage Loopers 73
- Colorado Potato Beetle 76
- Flea Beetles 79
- Mexican Bean Beetle 82
- Japanese Beetles 87
- Thrips 90

CHAPTER 10 – Planning Your Garden 95

- Companion Plants 95
  - Achillea (achillea millefolium) 95
  - Garlic 95
  - Asparagus 96
  - Beets 97
  - Basil 97
  - Borage 97
  - Chamomile 98
  - Carrot 98
  - Cabbage 99
  - Kohlrabi 101
  - Chervil 101
  - Cucumbers 101
  - Onions 102
- Companion Crops 103
- Interspersed Crops 104
- Plant Combinations to Avoid 105
  - Dandelion 105
  - Beans and Green Beans 106
  - Beans and broad beans (Phaseolus e Viciafaba) 106
  - Beans and Potatoes 107
  - Strawberry 108
  - Buckwheat 109
  - Maize 109
  - Lettuce 110
  - Lupin 110

Eggplant 110
Nettle 111
Potatoes 112
Peas 114
Tomato 114
Leeks 115
Parsley 116
Oak 116
Radishes 116
Roses 117
Celery 118
Celeriac 118
Marigold 119
Valerian 120
Pumpkins 121

CHAPTER 11 - How to create the Compost 123

How to make Compost 124
How to compost using the composter 128
A DIY composter 129
Odorless Compost with Japanese fermentation 130

CHAPTER 12 - Crop Rotation 133

Soil Tiredness 133
The importance of crop rotation 135
Various crop rotation systems 136
Alternations According to Botanical Families 140
Soil set-aside and green manure 143
    Leguminous green manure 144
    The field bean green manure 144
Crop rotations in the home garden 145

CHAPTER 13 - Home for Useful Insects 147

How to make the insect-home 147
A "bug-caller" garden 150

CHAPTER 14 - Hydroponics Plantation 151

CONCLUSIONS 155

CHAPTER 1 - What is Companion Planting?

In life, there are some people who are compatible and form a good couple and there are people who are incompatible and cannot even stay in the same room without ruffling.

Plants are similar to people in this sense.

Some plants are compatible with each other and have traits that make them great partners, while other plants are incompatible and collide incessantly, leaving both plants exhausted and weak. Knowing which plants are good neighbours and which must be kept away from each other is the essence of growing together.

The consociation is a very ancient agricultural practice that consists in cultivating in the garden and especially in the same soil different species of horticultural plants that are not in competition with each other, but rather derive a mutual benefit from it, living in a kind of symbiosis.

To put it simply, planting pet plants means planting plants in the immediate vicinity, because they are able to help the plants around them. This could be done through the nutrients that one plant adds to the soil that another plant needs. It could be through the insects that a plant attracts that help its neighbours or it could be because a plant emits chemicals or has a scent that keeps pests at bay. It could also be something as simple as a taller plant that provides shade during the heat of the day.

Sometimes the help is one-sided, as in the case of trap plants are put in the garden to lure insects away from desirable crops. Other times, the plants benefit each other, as when a plant provides shade to a smaller plant and is rewarded by adding nutrients to the soil.

Companion plantings are not only useful for plants planted close together, but importantly, when combined with flowers and other types of ornamental plants they are naturally protected against pests and fungal diseases; in this way the garden will be healthy and why not also beautiful to the eye with seasonal blooms that with their colours create a truly unique spectacle.

Plantation in company allows you to take full advantage of these natural interactions between plants. Blackberries can be used to attract parasite wasps that prey on garden pests that feed on other plants. Clover and legumes can be used to fix nitrogen in the soil. Asparagus repels nematodes that attack tomatoes. Knowing what each plant in your garden is capable of allows you to create a plan in which each plant is placed in a position where it is more likely to thrive because it has neighbours that complement its capabilities.

As well as knowing which plants are good neighbours, it is equally important to make sure that plants that are bad neighbours are kept at opposite ends of the garden.

If you have been gardening without taking pet plants into account, you have it all wrong. Make life much easier for yourself by making life easier for your plants.

CHAPTER 2 - How to realize the Garden

The preparation of the land for the garden is as follows:

The first operation is certainly the most tiring, it is to spade all the soil, sinking the spade 15/20 cm. deep and turning the clods of earth. Then, with a rake with metal teeth, it is necessary to proceed with a careful raking in order to crumble the biggest clods (it is an important operation for the success of sowing) and, at the same time, to weed out the weeds and remove the stones. At this point you have to pass over the ground with a crusher roller, proceeding first vertically and then horizontally, then it has to be raked again (possibly with a metal rake with narrower teeth than the previous one), always checking and removing any weeds and stones, then you have to pass over the ground with the roller, obliquely, from left to right and vice versa. It is important that all these operations are carried out with the ground perfectly dry.

The soil thus tilled must be left to rest for a week, after which, after the usual check and eventual removal of weeds and stones, fertilization is carried out.

When choosing the fertilizer to be used, it is necessary to take into account the type of soil to be treated, scrupulously following the doses indicated on the package or suggested by the retailer: an excess of fertilizer does not improve the fertility of the soil, on the contrary, in some cases it can create problems. The fertilizer must be spread over the entire surface and then raked to allow easy penetration into the soil.

After about ten days, which are essential for complete absorption of the fertiliser, sowing can finally take place.

Before sowing, the area must be divided into rectangles (flowerbeds), each of which will be dedicated to a crop. The size of these flowerbeds will obviously depend on how much space you intend to devote to one vegetable compared to another. In order to do this job well, it is advisable to stretch some cords and follow them with the shovel by making small dividing digs.

For sowing it is always advisable to use new seeds and not to reuse those of the previous year, unless they are still packaged and the expiry date is indicated on the package. If sowing takes place in late spring or even in summer, it is good to wet the soil 24 hours earlier. At this point you can proceed with a small hoe, digging as long as the chosen flowerbed and a little wider than the width of the seeds you intend to plant. In this small row must be placed the seeds that, if they are large (beans, broad beans, etc..), must be placed one at a time, if their size is small (salad, basil, etc..) must be taken in the palm of the hand clenched with a fist and slipped between thumb and index finger folded.

To cover the seeds, you can use the same hoe, taking care to act with the utmost delicacy. Finally, at sunset you must proceed with a good rain wetting, an operation that will be repeated every day. The garden must be wet every day, without exaggerating the amount of water. At the first growth it is necessary to thin out the cultivation in order to avoid that the small plants suffocate each other; it is necessary to proceed with the extirpation of the sick or imperfect ones, paying attention, however, because the roots could have intertwined with those of the adjacent small plants.

When deciding which flowerbeds to allocate to the different crops, you must take into account the problems related to the "intercropping" of the various types of vegetables and herbs. It has been verified that the proximity of certain vegetables increases the speed of development, size and quality of the fruit. The most sceptical can verify the ancient technique of 'consociation' by sowing two rows of radishes, alternating respectively with a row of watercress and a row of chervil. The difference in the taste of the radishes that will grow will be impressive: while those grown near the chervil will be very spicy, those near the cress will be tasty, but delicate.

This same technique also helps to stem the problem of some pests, for example: the combination of carrots and onions is excellent both for the final quality of the fruit and because the onion keeps the carrot fly away and the carrot does the same with onion pests. Based on this principle there are also some herbs with an absolutely insect-repellent odour which, if planted around the flowerbeds to be protected or the entire garden, make an important contribution to pest control. Basil, for example, repels flies and mosquitoes; mint keeps the cabbage away; flax keeps the Dorifora away from potatoes.

Sun vs Partial Shadow

One of the most important decisions you will have to make will be to grow a garden in full sun or a partially shaded garden. The amount of sun and shade that an area gets is one of the main determinants of the types of plants that can be grown there.

Most fruits and vegetables prefer full sun, so if you are looking to grow a vegetable garden this is the way to go

That doesn't mean that all crops prefer the sun to the shade. Full sun is defined as at least 6 hours of sunlight per day, while some plants need at least 8-10 hours per day to thrive. Trying to grow plants that require more hours of sunshine in an area that receives less sun exposure will be a frustrating exercise. Plants can grow, but yields will shrink and be more susceptible to pests and disease attacks.

Partial shading means that a plant needs less sunlight and can survive 3 to 6 hours of sunlight per day. These plants produce better when in the afternoon sun shade. Placing a plant that prefers partial shade or partial sun in an area that receives full sunlight can burn the plant when temperatures start to rise, causing it to wither or even die.

Most vegetables, fruits and herbs prefer full sunlight. If you have a garden that receives only part of the sunlight, you will need to select plants that can be grown with only part of the sunlight. There is not much you can do to increase the amount of sunlight. Reflective mulches can be used to reflect sunlight back to the plants, but the effect is minimal.

Lettuce, spinach, radishes and some strawberry varieties are well suited to partially shaded garden areas. Other crops such as peas and potatoes will grow in partial shade, but yields will be reduced. To be clear, these plants will still need sunlight to grow: they don't need it as much as other more needy plants.

Those looking to grow plants that need partial shade in a sunny position have a handful of options available to them. First, you can build a structure that provides shade at certain times of the day. It is better to build a structure that provides relief from the afternoon sun instead of one that provides shade in the morning. The afternoon sun is warmer and can damage plants than the morning sun. Another option is to build a trellis through which the sun can shine. Your plants will receive sunlight all day long, but will not be exposed to the constant heat of the sun. Some plants will perform better than others with this technique, so experiment to find out what works best.

You may be wondering what all this has to do with sowing in a subsidiary. There are some plants that grow tall or have large spreading leaves that can be used to provide shade for smaller plants. Larger plants can be planted as companion plants to smaller plants that need partial shade. Corn, sunflowers, tomatoes and artichokes can be planted to provide shade for smaller plants. Trellis plants such as beans and grapes are also a good way to provide spotted sunlight, which is the light that is filtered through the leaves of the trellis plant.

These larger sun-loving plants can be planted to provide shade to plants like cabbage, broccoli and cauliflower that are not good when temperatures start to rise as summer approaches. Even smaller plants such as carrots, cucumbers and lettuce can benefit from being planted in the shade of a taller plant as long as the taller plants do not surround them.

Trees can be used to provide shade, but be careful not to use a variety of trees that will grow at great heights and completely block out sunlight.

Kevin S. Stevenson
Companion Planting for Beginners

CHAPTER 3 – Companion Planting Benefits

The pros of combining plants from different families are varied. The combinations with plants that function as natural repellents such as marigold and carnation, keep the plants in the garden healthy; the lovage stimulates their growth and development; others such as marjoram, valerian or rhubarb improve their taste, others such as cumin, also bring improvements in the nature of the soil.

For example, fruit trees are used to shade excessively sunny areas, while other tall trees such as laurel, eucalyptus, planted in duly spaced rows, are useful as windbreaks for areas of the garden exposed to strong winds.

The vegetable garden also benefits from the combination of crops characterized by a very fast vegetative cycle and those with slower growth; in this way the harvests will be satisfactory even in those small vegetable gardens. If in the same plot of land, you combine tomatoes with tufted or cut lettuce we could harvest both leafy vegetables in a few weeks and firm, fleshy tomatoes months after sowing. Another advantage of the combination not to be underestimated is to increase the fertility of some plants of the same species or even those belonging to different families such as Apple, Pear, Olive and Vine.

They can provide nutrients Some plants contain large amounts of nutrients that other plants need and can be processed in the soil to provide subsequent crops with these nutrients. Others add nutrients to the soil as they grow.

An example of this would be planting a plant growing on a trellis near a plant growing along the ground to make good use of both horizontal and vertical space. Corn can be planted with beans and beans can be trained to grow corn stalks.

They can reduce the amount of maintenance a garden needs by planting weed choking, reducing pests and relieving disease, the gardener's work will be much easier in the long term. This is particularly true for organic gardens, because pet plants are often the first and only line of defence.

They attract or repel insects. Some plants attract insects that are beneficial to other plants. Others repel pests.

Plants with deep roots can be planted close to plants with shallow roots. This allows you to sow plants closer together without having to worry about competing for water and nutrients.

The best companions fill the gaps in the needs of the plants around them. For example, carrots are sensitive to carrot flies, which are small flies that can detect carrots up to a mile away. When they find a carrot patch, they lay eggs that hatch into worms that dig through the roots of the carrot plant and can decimate a crop. The worst part of the carrot fly is that you may not know you have been attacked until you go to collect the carrots and find a bunch of small holes. Planting carrots between rows of onions or leeks can confuse the carrot fly and prevent it from picking up the smell of your carrots.

The basic aim of planting pet plants is to sow plants in the immediate vicinity for the benefit of your neighbours. Sometimes it is one direct benefit from one plant to another, while other times the plants are mutually beneficial.

How do you identify the companion plants?

The information in this book is meant to guide you in the right direction, but it is important to realize that what works in one garden may not be ideal for another. Every single garden is an entity in its own right and may have strengths and weaknesses that other gardens do not have. It is up to you to find out what works best in your garden.

Although the information in this book should point you in the right direction, don't be afraid to experiment and see what works best for you. Spend some time searching for good and bad companions and you will come across recommendations that are in stark contrast to each other. Some sources say that corn and tomatoes are good neighbours, while others say they must be kept at a distance. This difference is most likely based on personal experience and neither source is wrong. The reality is probably somewhere in the middle, with the couple working as partners in vegetable gardens where there are not many of the worms that corn attracts, while they are bad to have together in vegetable gardens with a large worm population.

The best advice I can give is to try with partners who seem attractive to see if they work well together. If they do, good. If they don't, switch to other mates to see if they work better. The only firm rule when it comes to planting a mate is that there are no firm rules. There are general guidelines to know, but it is up to the individual to determine what works best in his or her garden.

CHAPTER 4 - What Plants Should be Used in a Garden?

Assuming that not all crops are suitable for growing on the same plot of land, here is a list of the different species of plants that can be grown on the same plot of land.

Leguminous plants, such as broad beans, peas, beans and green beans, are well associated with cruciferae (cabbage of any kind), cucurbitaceae (pumpkin, zucchini, watermelon, cucumber and melon), umbrelliferae such as parsley, fennel and wild fennel, carrots, celery and parsley, as they enrich the soil with nitrogen thanks to their roots that can capture atmospheric nitrogen and fix it in the soil, also useful as green manure once they have completed their vegetative cycle.

The Rosaceae, apple, pear, cherry, peach, plum, almond, medlar, rowan, apricot, quince and strawberry, on the contrary, are well combined with asparagus, radish and rustic plants such as dandelion and nettle.

Chenopodiacea, chard, beetroot and spinach, plants without flowers, are associated with onion and horseradish, and often develop salty or nitrate rich soils.

Labiatae, oregano, basil, lemon balm, lemon balm, lavender, marjoram, marrubium, rosemary, sage, thyme, savoury, mint are associated with all other plant families.

The leek is a vegetable belonging to the Liliaceae family that if it is alternated along the rows or between the rows with carrots, onions and celery is unlikely to be attacked by the white fly and ringworm.

Garlic, a natural pest repellent, goes well with courgettes, beets, tomatoes, lettuce and strawberries.

Cruciferae or Brassicaceae, cabbage, watercress, rapeseed, turnip and radish, benefit when combined with tomatoes, climbing beans, spinach and strawberries.

Radishes are vegetables that are grown with the different varieties of lettuce in tufted or cut lettuce, with peas, tomatoes, parsley or chervil.

Asteraceae, the most common lettuces, cabbages, carrots, radishes, strawberries and fennel, are associated with those varieties with a medium-long growth.

CHAPTER 5 - The Herbal Association

The growing technique is effective not only for the best growth and quality of the vegetables, but also to protect them from pest attack. There are in fact some herbs with an absolutely insect-repellent odour which, if planted around the flowerbeds to be protected or the entire garden, make an important contribution to pest control. Basil, for example, repels flies and mosquitoes; mint keeps the cabbage away; flax keeps the Dorifora away from potatoes. Let us look at the main ones together.

Herbs	Effects
southernwood	Sow here and there in the garden. It can be combined with cabbage, which improves taste and development. It keeps the cabbage butterfly away.
Yarrow	As a border, on the paths and near the aromatic herbs of which the production of essential oils increases.
Garlic	It contributes to the growth and health of roses and raspberries.
Dill	It goes with the cabbage. He doesn't like carrots.
Absinthe	As a border it keeps the animals away from the garden, but its proximity is not good for any plant: therefore, it should be kept at the right distance.
Basil	It goes well with tomatoes, improving their taste and development. It repels flies and

	mosquitoes. However, it hates the rue and can't stay near it.
Chamomile	Excellent consociation with cabbage and onions: it improves the taste and development.
chervil	It can be combined with radishes: it improves their development and flavour.
Cumin	Sowing here and there in the garden: softens the soil.
tarragon	Useful throughout the garden.
Chives	Carrots can be combined with carrots: it improves their taste and development.
Wild fennel	Keep away from the garden. Most plants don't appreciate the company.
hyssop	Keeps the guinea pig butterfly away. It's associated with cabbages and vines. He doesn't like radishes.
Lamio White	It's associated with potatoes, from which it keeps insects away.
Lovage	Sow here and there in the garden. It improves the taste and robustness of the plants.
Linen	Carrots and potatoes combined with it improves its taste and development. Keeps the dorifers away from the potatoes.
Marjoram	It improves the scent of plants.
Melissa	It improves the taste and development of tomatoes.
Mint	It improves the taste and development of cabbage and tomatoes. Keeps the cabbage butterfly away.
Mentuck	Keeps out the buckthorn.
Nasturtium	It is very useful for radishes, cabbage and all cucurbits. sown under fruit trees keeps aphids and other insects away.

Petunia	It protects the beans from insects.
Purslane	It can be used to keep the soil covered under maize.
Horseradish	Sown in the amphibians of the potato beds keeps the insects away.
Rosemary	It's compatible with cabbage, beans, carrots and sage. Keeps out the cabbage, carrot fly and epilachna.
Rue	Sown near roses and raspberries protects them from insects. Hates basil.
Sage	It can be with rosemary, cabbage and carrots but not with cucumbers.
Savory	Improves the taste and health of beans and onions.
Marigold	It is one of the most active plants in insect control.
Tansy	Sown with roses, raspberries, under fruit trees, keeps flying insects away.
Thyme	Its smell keeps the guinea pig away.
Valerian	It's all right anywhere in the garden.

CHAPTER 6 - Organic gardening and Companion Planting

Doing organic gardening means taking care of the garden by giving some rules and paying special attention to plants and flowers. The focal point of the practice is to establish a relationship of collaboration and mutual respect with nature.

n the first place, as is well known, it is necessary to forget about pesticides and chemical fertilizers. However, this does not mean abandoning plants to themselves. Natural alternatives are permitted, always in the smallest possible quantities. In fact, the approach of organic gardening is preventive rather than curative. For the same reason, it is advisable to choose plant species suitable for the climate and characteristics of the garden, so that no special care is required.

Cooperation with nature is everything and there are numerous allies to whom you can ask for help in organic gardening. One example above all? Ladybugs! They are real portents in the fight against aphids. Everything in the organic garden is connected and this is how it should be: cooperation between different types of plants with each other, with insects and animals is crucial. Trying to grow plants in isolation may not be a good idea. However, it is advisable to keep a relaxed approach and avoid extremism.

The key to getting the biggest and best harvests from any garden is to make sure the plants have the best possible companions. This is especially true for the organic gardener, who does not have herbicides and chemical pesticides available. While traditional gardeners can run down to the local garden centre at the first sign of trouble and take a chemical cocktail that immediately eliminates most problems that arise, organic gardeners do not have the same tools at their disposal.

Herbicides and pesticides could be the easy way out of trouble, but the organic gardener can rest easy knowing that they are growing healthy foods that are largely free of chemicals. Traces of chemicals used in a garden can be traced back to the final product. Any pesticide or herbicide (or both) that has been used during the cultivation of a crop will make it into products harvested from the crop. In the grand scheme of things, a couple of pieces of contaminated fruit or vegetables will not do much harm, but the cumulative effect of daily consumption of contaminated products could.

The knowledge that the gardener will end up eating a small amount of just about everything he treats his plants with is the driving factor behind a large number of gardeners deciding to switch to organic. While there are clear health benefits of going organic, it makes gardening a much more difficult proposition.

One of the biggest problems for organic gardeners is the control of weeds and pests. When done well, buddy planting can be implemented in organic gardens to prevent pests from ever entering the garden. Pests that do enter are quickly eliminated by predatory insects in search of a quick snack.

You are planting an organic crop that will help another organic crop.

CHAPTER 7 - Allelopathy

Allelopathy is a phenomenon that occurs very frequently in interspecific and intraspecific competition between plants, both at the agro-ecosystem level and under natural growing conditions. The phenomenon consists in the release, through the radical apparatus, of substances that can inhibit the growth and development of neighbouring competing plants and in this case, these substances behave as radical phytotoxins.

Allelopathy can also be stimulated by certain parasites, which facilitate the production of such substances to prevent other parasites from interacting with the same host. In general, at the agro-ecosystem level, allelopathy reduces interspecific competition because it inhibits or hinders the growth of other plants potentially competing in the availability of resources (nutrients, water, light).

Allelopathy has been considered, for a long time, a negative phenomenon in cases of replanting, as it is part of the complex of phenomena at the basis of soil fatigue: due to the presence of radical toxins, several fruit species, in particular stone fruit, show symptoms of suffering when an orchard is replanted in succession to one of the same species.

In modern agro-ecology, this phenomenon, on the other hand, must be re-evaluated because it is that action that the ecosystem, included in the plant-soil integrity, implements to avoid phenomena of soil drying and loss of biodiversity.

Allelopathy should therefore be seen as a phenomenon that safeguards biodiversity, through feedback systems; moreover, the emission of radical exudates, as in the case of associations or rotations, is also proving useful with regard to the better organoleptic value of agricultural products obtained in conditions of lower crop specialization.

Allelopathy should therefore be understood as an ecological defence action to preserve greater diversity of the agricultural or natural dissipative system.

Allelopathy is defined as the ability of plants to influence other plants through chemical interactions. When this effect is beneficial it is known as positive allelopathy and when the impact is harmful it is known as negative allelopathy.

Perhaps the best-known negative allelopathy comes from the black walnut tree, which releases a chemical into the soil that prevents other plants and trees from growing around them in a radius that can extend up to 80' from the tree. Eucalyptus trees, other walnut trees and cotton trees can have a similar effect on specific crops, as can trees grown on black walnut rootstocks.

A number of invasive weeds are also highly allelopatic and can have an impact on plants planted nearby.

A raised garden can allow crops to be planted closer to the allelopatic trees than is normally the case.

CHAPTER 8 - Insects

Good and Bad

When you create a garden, you can count on it to attract a large number of insects. Some will be good; some will be bad and some won't make much difference one way or the other. Take note of both the pests and the beneficial insects that each plant is able to attract. Then select the plants that repel or eliminate pests that you know are likely to appear.

There are a handful of ways in which accompanying plants can be useful to your garden when it comes to both attracting and discouraging insects.

Some plants repel certain types of pests because they don't care about their appearance, smell and taste.

Some plants attract predatory insects that prey on garden pests.

Some plants act as "trap plants" that can be planted to lure insects out of the garden.

Some plants have strong scents that mask the smell of other plants that are susceptible to attack.

To understand how beneficial, it is to plant an insect control mate in a garden, let's pretend you are an aphid. The aphid identifies a patch of greenery, flies to the garden and stands on a plant. It is likely that the plant it lands on is the one it likes, because aphids suck the sap from most fruit and vegetable plants. Because aphids are capable of asexual reproduction, a single aphid landing on a plant in your garden could give birth to millions or even billions of aphids over a growing season. The ability of aphids to reproduce rapidly is the reason why your garden goes from a perfectly healthy garden to one that appears to be completely infested from one day to the next. They reproduce, suck out the sap until the plant on which they are found starts to dry out and then sprout their wings so that they can move on to the next plant.

Then, imagine a garden designed with pet plants to keep the aphids at bay. The aphid still flies over the garden and identifies it as a potential source of food, but this time it approaches and discovers that the garden is full of onions, garlic, marigolds, coriander, dill and other plants that repel aphids. If he is lucky enough to find a plant far enough away from these plants, he soon finds himself under attack from voracious predators who have been lured by the plants in the garden. Ladybirds and green laces roam the garden in search of a tasty little aphid for a meal. The aphid finds the garden a very inhospitable place and falls victim to one of the many predators that wander among its leaves and branches.

An additional level of safety can be the following: planting geraniums near the rose bushes because Japanese beetles are attracted by the roses to the geraniums, which then proceed to poison the beetles and kill them.

Another way in which pet plants can benefit from gardens is to act as green bait". The greener a garden is, the harder it becomes for pests to identify the plants they want to hunt. Scientific studies have revealed that pests are less likely to find the plants they want when surrounded by less desirable green plants. In fact, studies have shown that green plastic is an effective bait that can be used to prevent pests from landing in a garden.

Designing your garden to keep pests away and make them less likely to find your crops will give you a better chance of having a healthy garden. In order to plan a garden correctly, you need to have a good knowledge of what predators and beneficial insects will be attracted to and then take steps to eliminate pests.

Kevin S. Stevenson
Companion Planting for Beginners

CHAPTER 9 - Beneficial Insects in the Garden

Let's take a look at some of the beneficial insects you might be able to attract in your garden and why it's nice to have them around. Depending on where you live, you may not be able to attract all these insects, but you should be able to attract enough to make a difference.

Ask a local nursery to find out which insects are in your area. If not, you may be able to go to a local farmers market and get some good information. Look for farmers who sell organic vegetables, because they are usually more in tune with the local insect population. Conventional farmers tend to spray everything, killing all the insects in the process.

What useful insects are and how they work?

In this particular historical period, in which the problems created by the use of Phytosanitary products for the control of diseases and insects in agriculture have become known, organic control methods have become more and more evolved and established to reach levels of complexity and effectiveness that can replace traditional methods.

With the evolution of organic farming and the continuous search for alternative methods to common plant protection products has led to the development of control techniques derived directly from the observation of the environment and nature, and in the case of insect control, it has been seen that it is the insects, with their dietary behaviour, to help us to combat and eliminate pests from our garden and garden plants.

After years of research and development, the various specialized companies have been able to offer on the market these biological solutions, which are supplied in every state of development of insects, from eggs, through the larval state to the adult insect.

But how can we exploit these useful insects in our garden or vegetable garden to combat pests?

The first step will be to identify the parasites present on our plants, and the degree of infestation. We can also lean towards a preventive attitude, and figure out which pests usually infest our plants.

Once we have identified the harmful insect, we can start our web search to find the natural antagonist insect of the pest. We can find a multitude of insects specific to the most common pests, from Aphids to Cochineals, from Snails to Oziorrinco and Beetle larvae.

After choosing the antagonistic insects, we will have to choose which form to receive among eggs, larvae or adult insects. This choice should be weighted according to certain factors:

Period of insertion in the ecosystem of useful insects, usually the further away from the beginning of the pest infestation period, the more developed the useful insects will have to be.

Climatic and environmental conditions for the settlement of the insects should be favourable to the various forms of our friendly insects.

Presence or absence of parasites, as the feeding of our antagonist insects will vary according to their state of development.

Little or no use of insecticides that would harm the health of insects.

These conditions will be fundamental for the growth, development and settlement of the insects, which we can encourage by following certain measures, including the installation of a specific "den" for certain types of insects (e.g. ladybugs and nematodes) or the preparation of the soil where we will settle our multi-legged friends.

If we succeed in meeting these conditions, our army of insects will be available to fight the pests that infest our garden and orchard, without the use of insecticides and respecting nature and its natural processes.

Useful insects for gardens and vegetable gardens

Here is a list of some useful insects (and a brief description of their usefulness) perhaps the most common in our gardens: spiders, ladybugs, parasitic wasps, chrysops, scissors, predatory aphids, hoverflies and parasitic flies.

It is obvious that you should not use chemicals if you want to attract beneficial insects.

Some pollinating insects and parasites are very small and so love plants with small flowers.

Other flowers that attract this type of insects (and also bees) are tubular flowers like digital. If you look closely you will notice that the lower edge of the flower is the landing platform for the insect.

Include a mixture of plants in your garden, which bloom at different times of the year.

For example, in early spring witch hazel, calicans, hellebores and crocuses are in bloom, you will usually find pollinating insects that come out of hibernation and get busy. Other plants that provide food for insects in spring are Cornus mas (cornelian), winter wolfsbane (a bulbous), and Mahonia aquifolium.

At the end of the season instead provide them with food with echinacea, aster, golden rod.

Ladybugs

It is a very useful animal in the garden and is used in organic farming. It is able to lay as many as 400 eggs in the period of May. They feed on mites and aphids and often settle near the colonies of these parasites.

Ladybug larva

He is the aphids' greatest enemy. He can eat several dozens of them in a day. The ladybug larva, after having eaten a large quantity of aphids, turns into NINFA (and then becomes an adult insect, the ladybug we all know).

It will continue to eat aphids; it will mate and make a lot of eggs from which many larvae will be born that will begin to eat aphids ...and so on.

HOW TO ATTRACT LADYBUGS

Among the plants that particularly attract ladybugs are horseradish, cauliflowers and broccoli. It is therefore possible to consider enriching your garden with this type of vegetable in order to encourage the presence of beneficial insects. Ladybugs would be especially attracted by their aroma. When designing a synergistic garden, it might be useful to alternate rows of broccoli or cauliflowers with other vegetables. Another useful advice is to keep the stalks of cauliflowers and broccoli in the soil so that they can also play a beneficial role in attracting ladybugs after the vegetables have been harvested.

There are also aromatic herbs and flowers considered to be particularly capable of attracting ladybirds and predatory insects. It is therefore possible to organise one's own garden in such a way that in its vicinity, for example by creating flowering borders, or inside it, by positioning flowerbeds or creating dedicated clumps, there are grasses, flowers and other vegetables that are able to attract ladybugs and useful insects.

Among the flowers which will allow to avoid the utilization of toxic pesticides, as they are capable to attract the entomophagous insects (which nourish, that is, of other insects), among which, besides the ladybugs, may be inserted the hoverflies and the members of the families of the Hemiptera., diptera, beetles and neuropterans (all predatory insects), we find:

1) Marigold, able to attract hoverflies.

2) The potentilla, whose yellow flowers are particularly attractive for ladybugs.

3) The dandelion, also among the flowers loved by ladybugs.

4) The geraniums, which attract useful insects both because of their colours and their scent.

5) Cornflower, whose presence attracts hoverflies and ladybugs.

Among the plants and aromatic herbs with which you can enrich your garden and vegetable garden in order to attract useful insects and avoid the use of pesticides, you can identify them:

1) Nettle, a real natural pesticide useful against aphids.

2) Garlic, another natural pesticide that can be planted in rows in the garden.

3) Sage, which attracts bees and insects useful for pest control and pollination.

4) thyme, another essential aromatic plant for biological control; it attracts hoverflies.

5) Coriander, which attracts useful insects and can be inserted in flowerbeds.

Other plants considered useful to attract beneficial insects to the garden are the potentilla, the fennel, the dill, the yarrow, the yarrow, the angelica, the flowers of the genus Coreopsis, the common blackberry and the flowers of the genus Marigold.

In the biological fight against insects harmful to the garden and parasites, it can also be useful to use the plant associations that can act in synergy to protect against adversities. To cite a few reference examples:

1) Mint planted near tomatoes protects these fruits from pests.

2) Rosemary and sage protect vegetables such as carrots and beans from pests.

3) Linseed flowers keep the Dorifora away from potatoes.

4) Carrots and onions, planted next to each other, protect each other from pests.

5) Thyme, planted next to cabbages, helps to keep the cabbage butterfly away.

SYMBIOSIS BETWEEN APHIDS AND ANTS

Over the millennia an elation of mutualistic symbiosis between aphids and ants has been created:

1. the aphids provide the honeydew (sugary substance) that ants are so fond of.
2. Ants, in return, protect aphids from predators.
3. The ladybug, which is a voracious predator of aphids, is opposed and driven away by ants.

Aphids

Most of them are bred by some kinds of ants, which take care of them and carry them on tender twigs in order to feed them easily, and from which they "milk" the honeydew.

The honeydew is made up, in practice, of the aphids' droppings and is a sugary substance of which the ants are greedy.

How can we counteract this defensive system?

By preventing the access of the ants to the tree to defend, by tying a ribbon of paper covered with glue around the trunk, so the ants remain attached to the glue, and the tree can gradually recover from the attacks suffered.

Hoverflies

Hoverflies look a lot like bees and wasps. As the adults of the Hoverflies feed on pollen, nectar and honeydew, let's see which plants to grow in the garden to attract them.

Hoverflies are harmless and quite easy to approach: just open your hand and slowly approach them while they are flying. They are excellent flyers so much so that they can remain suspended in the air for several seconds and then resume their flight accelerating with surprising shots.

The adults of many species of hoverfly have a similar appearance to that of a bee or wasp.

Hoverflies, however, differ from bees and wasps in that they have only one pair of wings, very short antennae and because they do not have a sting.

Only the larvae feed on aphids.

The Hoverflies can be easily attracted in a small vegetable garden by creating in the four corners flowerbeds of herbaceous ornamental and medicinal plants, using, for example, marigold, cornflower, chrysanthemum, marigold and borage, generous producers of pollen and nectar.

Osmia

Osmia rufa is an apoid hymenoptera smaller than Osmia cuckold. It has a tawny (reddish-blonde) hair in its chest. The abdomen is also tending to blond. The horned osmia is an apothecary hymenoptera of variable dimensions between 12 and 15 mm. It owes its name to the presence, in the females, of two "horns" in the front part of the head, between the forehead and the upper lip, before the eyes. The males, on the contrary, have a characteristic white hairiness present at the level of the mandibles.

Nematode

Plant parasite nematodes (Meloidogyne, Ditylenchus, Globodera, Heterodera, etc.) are worms between 2 and 5 mm long, colourless, eel-like or otriform, which sting the tissues of the host plant. Some of them cause the formation of galls (genera Meloidogyne, Ditylenchus), others do not (genera Heterodera, Globodera).

They attack numerous horticultural plants belonging to the families Cucurbitaceae, Solanaceae, Cruciferae, Composite, Umbrelliferae, Chenopodiaceae, as well as strawberry, corn, tobacco and sugar beet; fruit trees such as vines, Pomaceae and Drupaceae; flowering plants; wild plants.

How the Nematodes are made

The adult female has a pearl-white sac-like body and lays up to 1000 eggs. The eggs, in the shape of an ellipse, are surrounded by a mucilaginous substance and are often attached to the rear end of the female in a gelatinous sac.

The males have a cylindrical and thin shape and are provided with a robust stiletto. The reproduction takes place by parthenogenesis.

What damage do the Nematodes cause?

They are forced parasites; they sting and suck the tissues of the plant that modify themselves giving rise to the formation of galls (the characteristic symptom of the infestation); while they sting, they can inject dangerous viruses into the parasite plant.

The attacked plants show a delay in vegetative development because the absorption of nutrients by the roots is reduced, poor quality and quantity production, increased susceptibility to the action of other pathogens, underdeveloped root system, yellowing and foliar withering, until early death.

The affected roots may be favoured by the establishment of mushrooms and bacteria that cause root rot.

In addition, nematodes cause indirect damage as possible virus transmitters.

When they hit the Nematodes

In the absence of host plants, during the winter, only larvae and eggs are found in the soil or in undecomposed roots.

Under favourable environmental conditions, soil temperature of 18-20 °C, optimal humidity and host plants, the eggs hatch and give rise to second stage larvae which penetrate the root tips, mute 3 times and reach maturity. After spawning, new larvae are born within 15 days and so on for up to 6 generations per year. In mild areas the infestation can begin in April and end in November.

How to prevent

Attention especially in areas with mild climate and sandy, light, irrigated soil.

Of the vegetable and fruit varieties cultivated, those certified resistant to galligenous nematodes.

Succession with non-sensitive plants or nematocide plants (bait plants such as oil horseradish or white mustard, which attract the larvae of parasite nematodes but block their reproduction).

Strengthen the roots of perennial plants by distributing a biological product with fortifying activity to the root system of the plants, thus making them more resistant to nematodes and soil mushrooms attacks.

How to fight Nematodes

The chemical means of administering nematocide substances to soil all require a patent.

Use biological means by burying Eruca sativa green manure, Raphanus sativus, Brassica juncea etc. in the infested soil, all plants that, when buried in the soil, release substances toxic to nematodes (bio-fumigation); the effectiveness is even greater by covering the soil with transparent plastic sheets that retain volatile harmful substances in the soil.

Fight them by physical means, through solarisation, which consists of overheating the soil using solar heat in summer, to ensure 4-8 weeks of effective heat treatment (the soil must be moist and then covered with transparent plastic sheets).

Praying Mantis

The praying mantis is an insect considered useful for our green spaces. Unlike parasites, in fact, it does not feed on plants, leaves or roots, but on other insects and larvae, giving us, from a certain point of view, a potentially lethal weapon for the other entomological species present in our gardens or vegetable gardens.

Everyone remembers the praying mantis because of a particular vice: that of eating its own male during the mating, but few actually understand its potentialities. This wonderful insect with its bright and intense green colour, is native to Africa and has spread naturally in southern Europe and Asia Minor with the passing of the centuries. It also arrived in North America thanks to an accidental import together with some plants destined for a nursery. The praying mantis is also known as the European mantis, it is 40 to 75 mm long, and its most curious physical feature is its front legs which are raised and joined like praying hands. They are in fact used to catch different types of insects, with which this specimen feeds.

The mantises lay their eggs in "containers", called ovoids, which they build themselves and attach to stones exposed to the sun. The neanids are born around May-June and reach maturity in August. As you well know, the female after or during the accompaniment devours the male from the head while the genitals continue their work. In any case, we are talking about an insect that is very easy to breed: it is even possible to make it live in terrariums furnished with live plants. Important: it only feeds on live insects. The praying mantis particularly likes locusts, green grasshoppers, crickets, but it has no problem eating spiders, beetles, flies, cockroaches and larvae.

Pollinating insects

Pollinating insects are fundamental within our ecosystem. By transporting pollen from one flower to another, in fact, they allow pollination and formation of the fruit.

Bees are certainly the best-known pollinating insects, but they are not the only ones. Bumblebees, flies and beetles also perform this function very well.

Pollinating insects, despite their fundamental work in our gardens and countryside, are at risk of extinction. This is due to the ever-increasing pollution, the reduction of their habitat and the abundant use of pesticides.

Features

As we have already mentioned, pollinating insects are all those insects that are not only found on flowers, but actively contribute to the pollination process. For this reason, they are also called pollinating insects, literally "wedding favouring".

From a morphological point of view, these insects develop according to different specialisations. However, they maintain common characteristics:

- sucking mug apparatus, specialized in pollen harvesting.
- body covered with thick bristles in which pollen can get stuck and transported
- elongated shape, able to reach the nectar

But what specifically do pollinate insects do?

They go from flower to flower to feed on nectar, a sugary element essential to their diet. The nectar is present inside the flowers in absolutely modest quantities, so as to force the insect to visit numerous plants before feeling full. The relationship between plants and pollinating insects is therefore absolutely mutualistic: food in exchange for fertilization.

The flowers are able to attract insects thanks to special characteristics, such as particular smells, bright colours, protective foliage and flowers with suitable shapes to facilitate entry.

Pollinating insects are divided into two large types:

- wild ones, like bumblebees
- those domesticated by man, like bees.

The orders of insects visiting the flowers are as follows:

- Lepidoptera, like butterflies.
- beetles
- hymenoptera, like bees, bumblebees or wasps.
- Diptera, like flies

Let's see them in detail.

The lepidoptera and the beetles

To the order of lepidoptera belong butterflies, which can be of two types:

- diurnal, characterized by wings with very bright colours and varied
- nocturnal, with darker-coloured wings known as moths

Lepidoptera have common characteristics: wings and legs as appendages of the thorax, presence of compound eyes, two pairs of membranous wings, a sucking mug apparatus called spiritromba (that is, a sort of long trunk which, in some species, can reach even 10 cm of length).

On the contrary, the beetles, even if they are not among the most present insects on the flowers, have been the very first pollinating insects from the evolutionary point of view.

The characteristics of beetles are as follows:

- hard exoskeleton
- hard front wings to protect the hind wings
- compound eyes
- mug chewing apparatus

Hymenoptera and Diptera

Within the order of hymenoptera we find the most known and abundant pollinating insects:

- bees
- the wasps, of which it is important to know their strengths and weaknesses. You can discover them here
- bumblebees

Hymenoptera, which we have specifically talked about in this article, are fundamental in terms of pollination of many fruit trees that may be present in your garden: cherry, peach, but they are just some crops that owe everything to their presence.

The bees are characterized by the presence of legs specially shaped for the collection and the storage of pollen, and have a very high and very specialized level of sociality; the wasps, on the contrary, integrate to the sugary diet of the small preys; the bumblebees are characterized by a yellow and black livery with bigger bands than those of the bees, and compared to the latter they are bigger and hairy.

As for the Diptera, the species present on the flowers are the so-called hoverflies:

- very similar to bees and wasps
- have only one pair of wings
- sucking mug
- aphids predators

The worst threat facing pollinating insects today is that of pollution.

Under normal conditions, pollinating insects, and especially bees, can smell flowers up to 1 km away. But due to the increasing pollution, this capacity of bees has been reduced: they can no longer smell the scent of flowers at a distance of more than 300m.

In addition, bees can potentially cover an area of 3km by collecting nectar left and right. In doing so, however, they unfortunately come into contact with a whole range of harmful products and pollutants.

Remember also that nectar taken from the flowers of treated plants undermines the health of all pollinating insects, especially the most sensitive ones: bees.

What can you do, in your own small way, to help these precious insects?

Attempting to help pollinating insects and understanding what can make a difference in your home garden or garden is a good practice to raise your awareness about safeguarding our ecosystem and biodiversity.

Here's how you can actually help the bees and all the other insects:

- plant them in your garden or on your windowsill, plants with plenty of nectar.
- through the laying of artificial nests, promotes nesting
- provide them with drinks, using a bowl with low edges.
- avoids the use of pesticides, fungicides and fertilizers

- support the local economy so as to reduce, albeit very little, harmful emissions linked to transport

Helping our pollinator friends is fundamental: by helping them you will be helping yourself and the well-being of the environment far beyond the gates of your garden.

Mealybugs

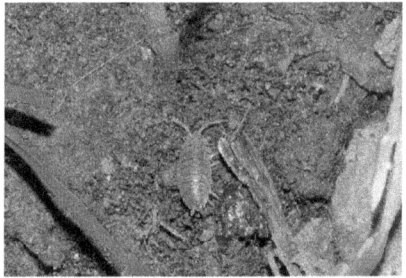

Only tiny cochineals from a tenth to a quarter-inch long do not seem particularly dangerous. However, these voracious plant suckers can literally suck the life out of your plants if you are not careful.

Today, I'm going to help you stop the cochineal manifestation on your plants forever. After reading the information below, you should know everything you need to get rid of these little pests and keep them out!

Cochineals are a parasite that slowly sucks the plants.

As part of the larger category of scale insects, scale insects are part of the Pseudococcidae family. These unarmed scale insects lack the semi-rigid or rigid shell of many other scale insects. Instead, the ladybug secretes a coating similar to defence wax.

There are over 2200 species of ladybugs, but only a fraction of them are considered common garden pests. Here is a short list of some of the most common garden pests.

Longlyeded Mealybug

A common greenhouse or nursery parasite. The name comes from the pair of long-tailed filaments that extend from the back and are often longer than its body.

The long-tailed floury insect prefers to dine on tropical plants such as bromeliads, Coleus, Croton or even the hoya plant.

Comstock mealybug

The Comstock Cochineal is common in the San Joaquin Valley area of California and deals mainly with lemon trees. Similar in many ways to citrus cochineal, it has a pair of medium length thorns protruding from the back.

Gill Mealybugs

Stone fruits such as apricot or peach are at risk of gill cochineals, as are some nuts such as pistachio or almond. Grapes and deciduous plants can also be at risk.

These fleshy pinkish insects are generally covered with white wax and may also have a cover of long crystalline filaments.

Obscure mealybug

Closely related to grape cochineal, the dark cochineal does not originate in California. However, it can be found there now, as well as South America, Australia, New Zealand and Iran, among others.

This long oval-bodied ladybug has small protrusions of filaments on its sides. Its white to greyish-white body is usually covered by a thick layer of white or off-white wax. These have many different hosts including various tuber, vegetable and fruit crops.

LIFECYCLE OF MEALYBUGS

With the exception of the long-tailed cochineal, the life cycle of the floury insect consists in an egg stage, a nymphal stage sometimes referred to as the "crawler stage" and the adult cochineal.

For the long-tailed floury insects, the life cycle is only the stage and the adult, as the female long-tailed cochineals give life to young.

Adult cochineals lay their eggs inside a cotton bag that protects them from the elements. This cotton mass is often mistaken for downy mildew.

Once the adult female has laid all her eggs, she will die. However, the average adult female can lay 300-600 eggs, making population growth surprisingly fast.

The eggs will hatch within 5-10 days in good weather conditions. Adverse weather conditions can cause a delay in hatching so that the egg sac can protect the young insects.

Dotted nymphs, or "crawlers", have vestigial legs and will move. This is the period of time in which cochineals travel and spread to other plants.

In agricultural situations where several plants of the same species are close to each other, it is common to see initial damage on the outer plants of a field. As the infestation spreads, the pests make their way inwards.

This crawler phase will last 6-9 weeks, during which time they mature and emerge as adults.

Females tend to remain stationary on their host plant (although they can still move, unlike other scale insects). Males do not feed after calving, so they will only live for a couple of days, mating with females they may find before they expire.

The cycle continues while the next series of adult cochineal females lay their eggs (or live young, for fleshy long-tailed insects), and then die. There may be several generations of floury bugs in a given year.

HABITAT

These parasites tend to live in and around what they eat. Different types will prefer leaves, stems, the base of the plant, roots and even the fruit in some cases as a home.

Some forms of scale insects accumulate in the leaf and stem joint, where they can have shelter from the elements. Others simply secrete extra protective wax and live openly on cactus pads or leaves where they are most exposed.

It depends very much on the particular species and plants where they are most likely, but it is very likely that an accumulation of wax secretion is visible, especially if eggs are present. On the plant you can also see cottony, glassy waxy filaments and egg sacs similar to cotton.

WHAT DO COCHINEALS EAT?

Depending on the mealybug species, you will find them in an increasing number of food crops, tropical plants and other ornamental plants.

Most of the mealybugs I have focused on are those common on fruit or nut trees or food crops. However, there are variations of cochineals that prefer ornamental plants or other trees.

For example, the cypress has a cochineal that will hide in the cracks and just below its mottled bark. There is a form of cochineal that also forms on cacti.

All cochineals consume the juice or juices of the plant to which they attach themselves. Usually they do not chew the leaves, but a large infestation can cause visible signs of yellowing.

Withered leaves and falling leaves are not uncommon. Fruit may fall prematurely and stunted plants may not be able to produce new leaves. A large enough infestation will cause the plants to die.

HOW TO ELIMINATE COCHINEALS

Ladybugs are attracted to plants with high nitrogen levels and, unfortunately, tend to include most of our valuable garden plants. So, what can you do to get rid of them? Here is a list of some of the best ways to get rid of them.

1. Organic cochineal control

Light and early infestations can be eliminated with cotton wool and a little alcohol. Simply dip the tip of the swab into the alcohol and punctuate the parasites. They will become extinct.

On succulent plants, you may find it easier to use a light mist of pure alcohol in a sprayer, but be careful how much you use. Too many things can damage the leaves.

Using a good insecticide soap can remove cochineals and remove egg debris. The soap passes through the outer waxy secretions and will damage the insect skin, causing dehydration and death. I recommend Safer Soap, which works on a large number of sucking pests.

A mycoinsecticide can also handle large-scale infestations. Products like Botanigard ES has a low-risk organic fungus in it. The fungal spores make their way inside the parasite insects and kill them, and the plants are not harmed. This organic method of cochineal control works surprisingly well.

2. Environmental control

Avoid excessive absorption and over-fertilisation. Plants that are too rich in nutrients tend to be high targets, as well as those that are saturated with many plant juices.

Blast cochineals and other insects from plants with a hard spray of water. While crawlers may be able to climb up plants, adults may not. They'll be extinct in a couple of days from starvation.

Make sure you have an abundance of beneficial insects that will help you control your cochineals. Ladybugs will eat the parasite eggs and nymphs.

An uncommon but equally effective beneficial insect is the cochineal destroyer, Cryptolaemus montrouzieri. These small beetles were originally transported to the United States from Australia in 1890 to help clarify citrus cochineal infestations. They are quite useful in greenhouses and outdoors and happily eat all stages of the floury insect's life.

3.   Preventing scale insects

To keep cochineals at bay, spray the plants once a week with a solution of neem oil in water. If you cover all the surfaces of the plants, the neem oil slows down or stops feeding on your plants with a wide variety of pests. In addition, the oil covers any eggs or tracks and suffocates them.

Because cochineals and ants have a symbiotic relationship, it is also essential to eliminate ants if you spy on them around your flesh. Keeping ants at bay reduces the chance of them being protected and cared for, which makes it easier to eliminate them altogether.

Green Lacewings

Green lace (scientifically known as Chrysoperla rufilabris) is widely used in various situations to control many different pests. Many species of adult lace do not kill pest insects, but actually exist on foods such as nectar, pollen and honeydew. It is their predator offspring that gets the job done. If you are looking for effective aphid control, green lace larvae should help do the trick.

The adult lacemaker lays eggs on the foliage where each egg is attached to the top of a hair-like strand. After a few days the eggs hatch and a small predatory larva emerges ready to eat some aphids.

The lace larvae are tiny when they emerge from the egg, but grow up to 3/8 of an inch long. They are known as aphid lions because they voraciously attack aphids by grabbing them with large jaws that suck and inject a paralyzing poison. The hollow jaws then extract the parasite's bodily fluids, killing it. Of all the commercial predators available, this lacemaker is the most voracious and has the greatest versatility for controlling aphids in field crops, orchards and greenhouses.

Each green lace larvae will devour 200 or more pests or pest eggs per week during their two to three week development period. After this stage, the larvae pupate by turning a cocoon with silk thread. About five days later, adult lace wings emerge to mate and repeat the life cycle. Depending on the weather conditions, the adult will live about four to six weeks.

Damsel Bugs

The Damsel Bugs are a family of predatory Heteroptera that usually feed on smaller preys than them. They can feed on a large number of insects and mites, thus helping to keep populations of different species of insects that are harmful to our vegetables stable.

Himacerus mirmicoides

In particular, they prey aphids, cochineals, mites, but also eggs of other families of insects such as butterflies and their larvae, for instance also the larvae of the cabbage, and it has been seen that they help also in controlling the populations of Lygus which nourish of numerous plants of our orchards. These small predators usually move on the grasses and low bushes, more rarely on the trees, and therefore are particularly useful in the vegetable gardens, where most of the plants belong to these categories. Like all heteroptera predators, they suck their preys with their rostrum, keeping them with the fore legs particularly adapted, so much that when they eat, they remind a little bit the mantids. Usually, they have only one generation per year, and the females lay the eggs in the hollow stems of several herbs. And here is one more reason not to keep the garden too "clean" from the "weeds". By sure, it is not that we have to leave all the spontaneous plants growing in the garden, otherwise many of the plants we cultivate would be suffocated. But not even make tabula rasa as many try to do.

Nabis punctatus

Prostemma guttula

The garden must look a bit messy if we want to maintain a biodiversity such that we have no major problems with pests. And when you have to clean a piece at the end of the cultivation to plant something, I suggest not to immediately compose the weeds that we eradicate but to simply pile them in a corner or use them for mulching so that any eggs can hatch instead of decomposing in the composter. Even so, perhaps with a little more time, the plants will decompose and then form humus which will enrich the soil.

Parasitic Wasps

Parasitic wasps are so ferocious and cruel that Charles Darwin used to say "I cannot believe that a benevolent and all-powerful God would have created Ichneumonidae (a type of parasitic wasp) with the specific intention that they would find food in the living bodies of caterpillars...".

This ruthless hunter is associated with one of the most popular science fiction monsters in the world, Alien. In fact, like the latter, many parasitic wasps also inseminate a host with an egg that once grown devours it.

Wasps use a variety of host organisms, such as spiders, caterpillars, or the larvae of other insects. The prey is stung and paralyzed (but not killed) by the wasp, which lays its eggs inside the poor victim. After the hatching of the eggs, the larvae of the "torturers" eat it slowly from the whole, leading it to a slow and painful death.

There are several famous species of parasitic wasps such as the Dinocampus coccinellae, which, after having laid an egg in the abdomen of the poor ladybugs, during its larval development transforms them into guardians of its cocoon.

Or the terrible Vespa pepsis, between 5 and 7 cm long, which uses the tarantulas as host. The wasp stings the spider by injecting a toxin that paralyzes it but does not kill it. It then injects its eggs and transports it to the nest. To grow, the larvae will feed on the spider's flesh, deliberately devouring it in non-lethal places (fat, muscle), ensuring fresh meat for more than a month.

These wasps go from leaf to leaf in search of cabbage worms, beetles and fly larvae, lepidoptera eggs, various pupae and adult insects.

Wasp larvae develop inside the host's body and eventually kill it. A female wasp can parasite for example 200-300 caterpillars (if you see a lot of white capsules on the back of a caterpillar, these are the wasp cocoons) in its short life.

They dine only on pollen and nectar, so that we can attract them with plants that grow with small nectar-rich flowers.

They also love to settle on the elderberry bark. The plants that attract parasite wasps: Achillea filipendulina, Achillea millefolium, Allium tanguticum, Anethum graveolens, Daucus carrot...

Spiders

Spiders are excellent allies for our garden, because they eat the insects that feed on our plants and vegetables. According to Rod Crawford, an arachnid expert at the Burke Museum of Natural History and Culture at the University of Washington in Seattle, spiders eat more insects than any other creature, more than birds or bats.

What does that mean?

That having a large colony of spiders in our garden, we would not need to use other pesticides, even if natural, or, at the limit, that we could make very little use of them.

That's why it might be a good idea to try to implement the arrival of spider colonies, ready to work for us and help us maintain healthy vegetables and plants. This could be the most sustainable solution, because it would mean leaving nature to take its natural course.

The trick, then, is to create a welcoming habitat for spiders in our garden.

The process is very simple and the solutions can be various.

Meanwhile, let's think about what these little living things need: a place to stay indoors without getting wet or where they can shelter from direct sunlight and, finally, a place where they can draw water without danger.

A very simple way to attract spiders, therefore, could be to add a layer of mulch, made of cut grass or dead leaves, between the plants. This will also help to keep the right amount of moisture in the soil for our vegetables, especially in hot periods like this.

Another method, less effective but still valid, is to let wild herbs grow around some vegetables. It doesn't mean, of course, leaving our vegetable garden in neglect, it means rather not eliminating all the weeds, leaving those necessary to create the natural habitat for spiders. Naturally, the herbs should be "pruned" so that they remain below the level of our plants or vegetables.

This we believe is the most natural way to protect the plants in our garden or vegetable garden. So, the next time you see a spider, think twice before you try to send it away!

Predator flies

One of the families of insects that most contribute to the control of the insect fauna is the family of Asilidae, predatory flies of various sizes, up to 3cm and over. They are all very fast and skilled in catching their preys on the fly, and are so strong, at least some species, to be able to overpower preys even 4 times bigger than them.

Also, because when they grab their prey they sting them with their mouthparts of the pungent-sucking type and inject a liquid with a neurotoxic component that paralyzes the prey, then the proteolytic component dissolves the internal tissues of the prey that are then sucked by our kindergartens in a fairly short time.

Kind of like spiders.

Often, they hunt from a fixed perch, from which they leave to catch preys that pass in a fairly wide range, which makes us think that they are endowed with an excellent sight and that just the sight is the main sense organ involved in the hunt.

Also, for this reason they like to find a perch in an open and bright space.

The hours when it is easier to see them hunting are the brightest and hottest hours of the day, when it is cooler, they usually hide among the thickest vegetation.

They are all elongated flies, with long legs suitable for catching preys on the fly, some are almost similar to dragonflies, which are among the strongest predators of the air among the insects.

Obviously, a form of evolutionary convergence due to a very similar diet.

Not much is yet known about their biology. The spawning takes place in various ways. Some lay their eggs elongated on various plants, others release more spherical eggs scattered around, others lay eggs in the ground, or even under the bark or in decaying parts of trees. It seems that some larvae in the early stages of development do not feed except on the resources of the egg.

Others appear to behave as ectoparasites of other insects or insect larvae. Until some that in the final stages of development become true micro predators. It seems that some also feed on decomposing organic matter or plants.

The development of these larvae can last from a few months to almost three years, during which time they contribute to insect control perhaps more than as adults.

They hibernate as pupae from which the adults emerge in spring. Among the adults, females are the most engaged in hunting, probably because they obviously need more protein than males to produce eggs.

Sometimes it is easy to confuse kindergartens with horseflies.

One passes in the garden and suddenly a very agitated fly buzz around it.

It's easy to think of evil. Instead, at times, we have only passed close to a perch, and if we have the patience to observe for a moment, we will see the fly settling down again, and if we approach it very slowly and without dropping our shadow on the fly, we will be able to recognize that we are dealing, on the contrary, with a very useful guardian of our garden.

As usual, it is a matter of learning to observe with a little attention. Instead of immediately starting to give the air a few shots.

And if it really is a horsefly, standing still will make it rest on us giving us the opportunity, if you want, to eliminate the nuisance with a quick blow of the hand.

We can deduce several things from the biology of these insects. That, for example, those who make the heaps on which to cultivate if they also use rotten wood will favour some kindergartens, that if you can avoid spading more eggs than those that are scattered around, in short, as usual it is not to do the garden with the mania to keep everything clean, but with a little 'attention to all those who live there.

If we want to have a garden that doesn't need too many interventions. Because every time we change the living conditions of the inhabitants of our garden, we provoke a sort of cataclysm. Which in the long run creates imbalances that we will have to remedy. If we take care of ourselves, we can learn to avoid the biggest mistakes. And having a healthy garden without any subsequent intervention, which for me is always an indication that something was wrong.

Common insect pests

Aphids

Aphids are among the most known and feared by farmers.

There are numerous species, some specialized for some plants, others more polyphagous. They have very complicated reproductive methods that I will not describe now, who wants can easily find this information on the net.

As usual, what I am most interested in communicating is how to defend against these parasites, not when there are already too many of them, but how to avoid them becoming a problem.

They are not always an easy problem to solve. Obviously, as usual, it is very important to try to maintain maximum biodiversity.

In fact, there are many predators of aphids, and even if some are more incisive than others in controlling these insects, the set of all predators that can feed on aphids generally avoid those real invasions that are well known to anyone who has cultivated a vegetable garden.

One of the main problems when we try to control aphids is that most predators always arrive after the aphids have already reproduced in abundance.

One solution may be to wait with sowing, for example green beans, until there are already enough predators able to control the aphids, as I have described here. But we can also try to anticipate the arrival of our own. We must learn to observe not only our garden but also the vegetation around us. Almost always aphids appear first on some plants, which will also be the ones on which their predators and parasites will reproduce before on others. Here, for example, the plants on which the aphids arrive first are the Rumex pulcher and the Salvia officinalis, but obviously elsewhere they may be others. The important thing is to observe which ones they are. And make sure that they are always present in our garden.

So, at the beginning of spring we will favour all predators of aphids that feed on aphids both at larval and adult stage, such as ladybugs for example.

But there are many species of insects which nourish of aphids only in the juvenile stages, and which, when adult, nourish of other, such as, for instance, the Diptera Hoverflies, which, when adult, nourish of nectar, and in some cases also of pollen, whilst the larvae of some of them are really excellent predators of aphids.

In this case, it is not sufficient that there are the aphids, it is necessary that there are also the flowers which the adults nourish of, and I have already talked about this here.

Practically the same goes for those Braconid hymenoptera that parasitize aphids.

Another group of insects that boast different species of aphid predators are the Mirids (Miridae).

There are also many generic predators that are not particularly specialized in aphids, but which also contribute to the control of aphids, such as the smaller species of Asilidae, for example the genus Dioctria, or the smaller species of dragonflies, such as the Coenagrion.

But there are not only insects that prey on aphids. Many spiders can feed on aphids, and even the larger species such as the Argiope bruennichi, contribute greatly to limiting their spread. On the canvases of this beautiful species I have often seen many aphids entangled. Obviously, the spiders which fabricate cobwebs usually capture only the winged forms of aphids, limiting more than anything else their diffusion.

For this reason, the hedges around the garden are particularly useful, but also between one flowerbed and another, as a matter of fact, the hedges are the support on which many spiders fabricate their webs, and especially on the hedges, spiders often attack the ovisacs, those species of cocoons full of eggs which are used to make several species of spiders get through the winter. And then there are many species of spiders that do not make webs but search every stem, leaf and twig from ground level to the highest treetops, such as Salticidae, Philodromidae and many others.

In addition, the hedges also offer nesting possibilities to various insectivorous birds, such as blackcap, Sardinian warbler, Cince and others.

Especially for the tits I built nest houses that these prolific little birds love very much. And it's not easy to imagine how many insects a couple of Cince can take out if you haven't seen them doing in and out continuously for days and days on end. But there are still many more predators of aphids, so let's go back to the usual speech, that is to try to increase the biodiversity in our garden as much as possible, and a well-kept garden, in the sense that I try to explain in these pages, has easily a biodiversity greater than a natural environment in the same place. In fact, we can also plant flowers that in the natural environment around us are not there to attract those species that interest us.

One last word about plant associations.

We know that there are plants that love the proximity of other plants, for various reasons.

There are several "famous" associations, such as carrots - onions or kale - tomatoes, just to give two examples. In the case of carrots these are repellent to onion fly and onions are repellent to carrot fly. But I sometimes use a different kind of onion fly repellent which is perhaps a little less obvious. For example, I plant corn next to various plants for various reasons that I have already written about here. One of the reasons is that especially ants that breed aphids generally prefer to breed them on corn than on many other species of plants.

It's true that corn doesn't do very well in that case, but given how little it costs us to sow a little corn among the other plants that generally remain unharmed, I think it's a system to try. In the worst-case scenario, if the aphids become too many, we can eliminate the most affected maize leaves and thus kill a large number of aphids with very little effort.

Asparagus Beetles

The biological cycle of the asparagus cryocera includes the following stages: egg, four larval stages, one pupal stage and the adult beetle.

The adult asparagus cryoceris (Crioceris asparagus) have a bright blue head, black antennae and red chest. The elytras have two characteristic rows of white or yellow spots. The eggs are oval and black to brown-greenish in colour, arranged individually or in rows of 3 to 10 eggs perpendicularly on the branches and leaves of the asparagus plants.

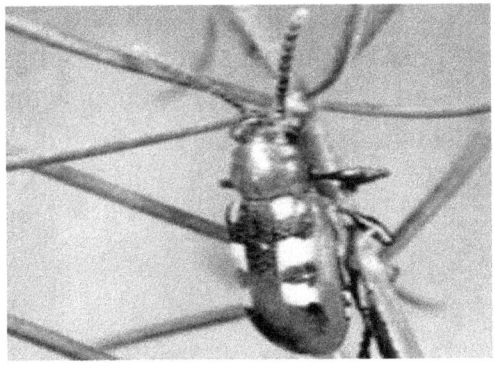

The larvae vary in colour from dark grey to whitish, have small black heads and three pairs of strong light brown legs. Once they reach full maturity, the larvae fall to the ground and become pupae. During the adult stage they hibernate and start a new cycle the following spring.

Symptoms of damage

Both the adult specimens and the larvae feed on the asparagus leaves. While the larvae feed, they secrete a blackish fluid consisting of faecal material, which soils the plant.

How to get rid of asparagus beetles

In most cases, organic treatment for asparagus beetles is recommended, unless the populations are huge or the asparagus plants are in serious danger. As soon as you notice asparagus beetles, start picking them by hand every day, throwing them into a bucket of soapy water. If you see brown eggs on the spears, be sure to peel them too.

Cut the asparagus while they appear and leave no more than two days between harvests can help prevent the eggs from hatching. Even if the spears are contaminated with eggs, cut them as soon as they are big enough to be collected.

Neem oil can be applied to plantations that have severe infestations, especially in years when harvesting is not recommended. Cover the spears well, applying neem to new spears every week. Picking berries at the end of the season can help keep asparagus beetles at bay.

If the asparagus beetles on the plants are severe and immediate control is needed to save the asparagus, both pyrethrin and malathion can be used without causing serious damage to useful insects. These chemicals are short-lived, last only a few days, but are potent. Beetles that keep coming and come across an asparagus path can be repelled with permethrin, but know that this chemical has a much longer life span and will kill most of the insects that come into contact with the asparagus medium.

Natural enemies

Hymenoptera can be used for the natural fight against asparagus cryocera: Tetrastichus coeruleus and Tetrastichus asparagus.

Cabbage Loopers

Cabbage Loopers (trichoplusia ni) is not only a harmful parasite of the cruciferous, their favourite guests, but can also be present in other crops such as tomatoes, peppers, some cucurbits, soy, sesame and cotton. One of the reasons why this parasite can be harmful is that the adult is able to disperse considerably, reaching distances of up to 200 km.

Biological cycle and appearance of Trichoplusia ni

Adults can lay up to 300 eggs in the lower margins of the upper leaves of the plants. The eggs are spherical in shape, with the flattened part attached to the leaf, and yellowish white or greenish. The larvae hatch after 3-4 days. As their legs are confined to the front and back of the body, they move "in a compass". They take from 15 to 20 days to pass through the 5 stages, changing colour from yellowish green to light green with a white band on both sides of the body. The transformation in pupa takes place in cocoons of sericeous filaments, often located in the lower part of the host plants. The pupa is green in colour and then become coffee brown when the flicker of the adult specimens' approaches. Finally, the adult specimen is grey-brown mottled with a silvery eight-shaped pattern on the front wings. The adult specimens live for 10-12 days.

Symptoms of damage

The caterpillars feed mainly on leaves causing irregular holes. In the first three stages they create small holes, while in the following stages they feed on the tissue between the veins skeletonising the leaf. They have a voracious appetite and can consume up to three times their body weight daily. The plants can be severely defoliated and rachitic.

How to get rid of the guinea pig

So, what are the tools in the farmer's hands to protect the crop? We see five effective defence methods for insect control.

Insecticide

The simplest and most resolutive method is the application of insecticides when the first generation appears. To monitor the presence of the lepidoptera, pheromone traps must be set up in the field in order to intercept the first flickers.

There are many registered pesticides on the market that can be used against cabbage and night cabbage. However, care must be taken because not all species of cabbage are registered for the same product. Therefore, care must be taken with the label.

Bacillus thuringiensis

An insecticide of biological origin based on Bacillus thuringiensis, a bacterium capable of killing this insect, is also effective against cabbage larvae in the early stages of development. The larva, in fact, when it ingests the bacterium deposited on the leaf, undergoes a blockage of digestive activities which causes its death in a few days.

Parasitoids

There are species of Diptera and Hymenoptera able to parasite Pieris brassicae and Mamestra brassicae. The most effective against the guinea pig are Trichogramma evanescens, which parasitizes the eggs, and Apanteles glomeratus, which instead affects the larvae, as well as Phryxe vulgaris. As for the noctua, there are some entomophages such as Amblyteles armatorius and Compsilura concinnata.

However, these are insects which are not commercialized, but which are present in nature and can play a role in the control of the parasite. It is therefore necessary to encourage their presence by, for example, taking the utmost care in the placement of any insecticides.

Cold

Perhaps the most harmful generation of cabbage is the last, because it develops in late summer-early autumn, when there is a lot of biomass in the field and the cabbage is practically ready for harvesting and marketing.

In the contrast of the last generation an important ally is frost. It is good practice to always monitor the weather forecast and in case of night frosts there is a good chance that most of the specimens will succumb to the cold.

Crop rotation

To avoid excessive pressure from these lepidoptera, it is good practice to allow at least four years to pass between the cultivation of one species belonging to the Cruciferae family and another. In this way the wintering chrysalis, once out of the ground, will not find food and will survive only in limited numbers.

Colorado Potato Beetle

The insect beetle, scientific name Melolontha melolontha, is a polyphagous beetle, that is capable of feeding on different substances; considered a parasite, it is particularly widespread in northern Italy. The "Beetle" is widespread especially in spring and May, hence the name. The adult beetle is 20-30 mm long; it is elongated and has a reddish-brownish elliptical colour and a dark chest (brown-blackish). Triangular in shape is the terminal part of the abdomen. The larvae (about 40 mm long) are whitish, practically similar to dogs and larvae in general. They nest in the soil and feed on roots, especially the tender consistency. The adult insect beetle feeds on leaves, which is why in periods of great infestation the damage to crops is considerable. The root-feeding larvae are equally harmful and block plant growth.

The fight against the insect beetle only takes place in cases of severe infestation and a large number of adults in flight. More complex is the fight against the larvae, which proliferate at about 20-30 cm in the ground undisturbed, and must be eradicated with special products. Prevention and interventions to eradicate cockchafers and larvae are implemented especially in nurseries. As a rule, the populations of insect beetles, both at the adult and larval stage, are controlled by numerous predators, such as crows and cuckoos for example. This fight by means of "natural enemies" is also carried out by man in less serious cases of infestation. Chemical and biological fight, on the contrary, is directed to the most serious cases, and products to be vaporized on the tops of the plants, on the leaves, or with especially granular products to be mixed in the mould, are used.

Natural enemies

There are several natural enemies of the insect beetle, such as some species of birds, which feed on both adult insects and larvae. Farmers or nurserymen will bring these animals to the place of cultivation, following strict forestry rules, if those already present are unable to eradicate the beetles. Some Diptera are also considered natural enemies and feed on the beetle larvae. In recent years, man-made but natural methods of defence are being experimented, which include the use of the fungus Beauveria brongniartii. This will be administered in the form of a preparation, and is allowed only in some areas. It can be administered to the plant both on the foliage and in the soil. Other gelatinous compounds include the use of Heterorhabditis.

Preventing damage

Preventing damage from the insect beetle is possible. The ground must be turned over often, so that beetles finding the soil too soft will avoid laying eggs in it. To keep adult insects away, you can equip yourself with a "bat box", a small house for bats; these are greedy for beetles. The neem oil, organic insecticide, on the contrary, is utilized on the larvae when their presence is already numerous, but it can be utilized also as a one-time prevention, pouring it directly into the soil. Pouring into the soil some mushrooms, like those mentioned in the previous paragraph, helps to prevent the infestations of beetles; in case of larvae already present, they will be eliminated in short time. In general, it is always better to use natural, and not chemical, products or methods for prevention, and always follow the laws and rules in this regard.

Flea Beetles

The nettles are also called land fleas or garden fleas, they are small dark coloured insects, only a few millimetres long, belonging to the family of beetles.

They are a phytophagous insect, which means that they feed on parts of the plant, in particular they love cabbage plants. In case of attack, even if it is not easy to see the tiny insect, it is easy to recognize the damage it causes: many small holes that go to prick the leaves.

The nettles generally strike young plants, going to eat the leaves. In particular they attack the species of the cruciferous family, such as cabbage, cauliflower broccoli, rocket, turnip tops and radish, or beets (ribs and grasses).

In the specific, there are two species of flea beetle that we often find doing damage in our vegetable gardens: the cabbage nettles (Phyllotreta nemorum), 2 mm long, with a yellow stripe, and the nettles of the beets (Chaetocnema tibialis), completely black and even smaller.

Feeding, the adult fleas create small holes easy to identify, then they lay the eggs in the ground, the larvae are harmless but grow up quickly, and once adult, they come back to eat our vegetables. These land fleas reproduce at a rate of two generations per year.

How to defend the garden

As for all harmful insects, there are various levels of defence from the flea beetle to be put in place, always with a view to organic farming. We can therefore implement cultivation techniques of prevention, annoy the insect to keep it away, or try to exterminate the population of parasites. It is always essential to intervene in good time, without passively allowing the problem to spread.

The first level is prevention: obviously avoiding the problem would be the best solution and a series of precautions can help, decreasing the possibility of significant damage by this parasite.

Prevention. In order to prevent the hives, crop rotation is important in the first place; in particular, it is not necessary to repeat on the same plot of vegetable garden crops that these fleas like. In this way we make life difficult for the beetle, preventing it from establishing itself in an area and continuing to find a plant to its liking. Frequent irrigation also keeps the flea beetle away from the plants in the garden, as they hate damp soil. Mulching, on the other hand, is useful in blocking the road to spawning, causing the insects to move.

The non-intervention. If root vegetables, such as radish, are grown, the damage of the flea beetle becomes negligible, also because it is a short-cycle vegetable. We can therefore decide the peaceful solution of letting the insect feast at the expense of the leaves, limiting ourselves to wet the crop very often in order to annoy and maybe drive away the parasite. This method only applies if there are no other target plants in the area, which could become the new object of flea attention.

Repellent and insecticide methods

Repellent methods. For small earth flea infestations, vegetables can be dusted with rock meal such as bentonite, or algae limestone, these methods form a mechanical barrier that discourages the insect and can act as a repellent. This is an excellent way of avoiding the use of insecticide.

Insecticide methods. If there are many insects, repellents are not enough and it is better to intervene to kill them. In this case we can use various products permitted by organic farming to combat them. The most effective is pyrethrum, it is a product of natural origin able to kill them, but to be used with great care as it could also kill useful insects. Other treatments with less environmental impact are the nettle macerate, which also has the advantage of being self-produced, and neem oil.

Mexican Bean Beetle

The Mexican Bean Scrabble looks a lot like a ladybug of a different colour and we all love ladybugs, or as some people call them. But underneath that pretty orange look is a voracious agricultural parasite. Unlike its sweet red relatives, it is not prey to other pests, but to the plants themselves. How can you avoid this hungry spotted beetle?

Mexican life cycle Bean Beetle

An adult beetle beetle laying eggs.

In late spring, Mexican bean beetle adults emerge from their dormant wintering state. The females begin laying their eggs in groups of 50-75 on the underside of the leaves.

The larvae feed quickly throughout the field as they hatch, devastating your crops. This period is when the worst damage occurs. As they grow, they go through four moulting cycles, removing the previous skin to allow further growth. Once they are at their full larval size, they will attach to the underside of a leaf. This whole cycle lasts 3-5 weeks.

Once they emerge from the pupa, the adult can begin the life cycle again. When the climate becomes cold in late autumn, they will retreat to the shelter of the local woods or hide in vegetable waste for the winter.

Habitat

Chewing the leaf tissue of the bean.

As the name suggests, it lives throughout Mexico and can be found across the Eastern United States. It also blooms in irrigated farmland west of the Rocky Mountains. Like most pests, they go where their food supply is most abundant.

They can be found during spring, summer and early autumn. The most destructive time of year for these Mexican beetles is summer. So, they retreat to a sheltered place in the nearby woods or under nearby plant debris for the winter.

What do they eat?

The lower part of the leaf has been decimated by this pesky parasite.

True to their name, they love leaves and bean pods. They will eat common beans, lima bean, green bean, soybean, adzuki bean, cowpeas, alfalfa and some clover. When they eat, they tend to skeleton the leaves, leaving visible damage behind. This makes it a little easier to notice the danger lurking under the foliage and take steps to eliminate bean beetles.

How to get rid of Mexican beetles

So now that you know all about them, let's explore ways to wipe these pesky Mexican bugs off your yard.

Organic control

Your first stage of defence is literally getting insects off your plants. Using your fingers or a pair of tweezers, remove the adult and larval stages from the leaves and throw them in a bucket of hot water and soap. This prevents adults from flying away and will kill the parasites. You can also use a flat object like the back of a butter knife or the side of a trowel to scrape eggs from the back of leaves if you discover a widespread collection. It is easier to cut the colonised leaves and destroy them completely.

I use diatomaceous earth not only to discourage spawning, but also to kill beetles. Their soft undersides do not match the sharp edges of fine crystalline powder. Diatomaceous earth for food use is completely safe for both humans and pets, but for insects it is like thousands of tiny razor blades.

Spot treatments with insecticidal soaps e.g. Safer Soap are good. If you see limited amounts of beetles in your yard, this should help sweep away what's there and discourage a longer stay. However, to make it effective you will need to carefully coat both the top and bottom of the leaves and the stems of the plants.

Neem oil can also be an effective means of control. While this is less likely to kill adults, it will prevent them from laying eggs on the covered leaves and will slowly poison the bean beetle larvae. It is even more effective when mixed with an insecticidal soap like Safer Soap. Neem oil also helps with other types of infestations such as aphids and grasshoppers.

Another option is to use pyrethrins. Your first choice should be Safer Garden and Garden Spray, which contains a mixture of potassium salts of fatty acids and pyrethrins. It works against a number of pests including cabbage worms, spider mites, cabbage loops and many others.

If the problem persists, opt for a stronger pyrethrin spray such as PyGanic. Follow the manufacturer's directions to deal with a serious infestation and you should be rewarded with a bunch of dead adult and larval insects.

Environmental Control

You might think it's weird to use a ladybug to check on a relative of the ladybug. However, in this particular case, it works quite well. Ladybugs prey on insect eggs and are not picky. Whether it's aphids and their eggs, yellow beetle eggs or any other insect, they will eat them. These insects will really help with most other forms of parasites.

Another beneficial insect that is great is lacewing. These little green insects will be happy enough to help you devour your eggs and beetle larvae, and they won't harm anything in your garden.

The tiny pirate bug can also be a great beneficial insect to convince you to stay in your garden. These will help keep the buzzer parasite population down while they're still killing your Mexican pests.

Barbed Soldier Bugs are also great beneficial insects and they also love to eat all kinds of pests, from bunches of eggs to the adult stage. They can also help you with your potato bug or Cutworm infestations.

Tips for prevention

Keep the beds free of plant debris from autumn throughout the winter. Debris, fallen leaves and the like make an excellent winter shelter for beetles. By keeping the area clear, you won't have unwanted guests in the long term.

Planting early ripening bean varieties can be a way to reduce the destruction of these pests. While Mexican bugs have been present in previous months, they are still coming out of hibernation. An early ripening variety can be well established and able to manage the damage before the bean beetle infestation. Also, bush beans are more resistant than polar beans. If you choose to plant beans instead, you may be able to reduce the population simply by that.

Using Harvest-Guard, for example, can help you keep all kinds of pests away from your plants. In addition to Mexican beetles, row covers can keep other species of beetles at bay. Cucumber beetles, asparagus beetles and flea beetles are deterred by this method. It will also help you prevent a number of other moth larvae such as the army worm or tomato worm.

Apply a light dusting of kaolin clay, sold commercially as Surround WP. This superfine clay forms a waxy coating on the surface of the leaves, deterring pests from eating them or placing them on top.

Choose to grow pet plants such as rosemary or marigold. These plants can help prevent pests from initially colonizing your backyard. Other plants that can work well for this purpose are nasturtium or summer salt.

Japanese Beetles

The popillia japonica, popularly known as the Japanese beetle, is a harmful insect very similar to the beetle. It was first sighted in Italy in 2014 and arrived accidentally from Japan due to human activities. Just as happened with the Tiger mosquito that arrived from abroad, in the form of eggs and/or larvae, in car tires containing tinned water.

For now, it is present only in some regions of Northern Italy, but if the infestations are not contained, it will soon spread to the Centre-Southern.

It has recently been added to the insects dangerous for the Italian plant heritage. In the list of dangerous insects, recently added we point out:

- the chestnut tree cynipid
- the red palm awl
- the Asian bug
- the chambermaid of the horse chestnut tree
- the Asian woodworm

Life Cycle

The adults come out of the ground between the end of May and the beginning of June, when temperatures start to rise. Between July and August, Japanese beetles move in large groups and never as isolated individuals.

By the end of the summer, the females lay their eggs under the grassy meadows and uncultivated fields.

The Japanese beetle overcomes the winter period in the form of larvae of different ages. It is in the form of a larva that feeds on its roots and becomes an adult insect in spring, with

How to recognize it

How to recognize the Japanese beetle? The adult insect resembles the classic beetle but is distinguished by the typical white dot on its side. In particular, it can be recognized by the presence of five spots of white hair on each side and, a larger spot, in the terminal area of the abdomen.

The body is on average 10 mm long, with bronze reflections on the back and has 12 tufts of white hairs: five on each side of the abdomen and two wider on the terminal part.

It is thanks to these "white dots" that it is possible to discriminate Popillia japonica from the classic Beetle that it is missing.

Damage and plants at risk

In the USA there are about 300 botanical species attacked by the popillia japonica.

In our country, the plants most at risk are:

- the maple trees
- lime trees
- elm
- grasses
- pink
- wisteria
- other ornamental plants
- apple tree
- peach
- screw
- Actinidia
- core
- other fruit plants
- corn
- soya
- other extensive field crops
- tomatoes
- other vegetables

Fight and Remedies

The fight against popillia japonica uses three different strategies:

- manual beetle capture
- capture by pheromone traps of adult insects
- biological control by introducing the natural predators of the popillia japonica in every moment of its life cycle (adult, larva or pupa)

Biological control has been very effective in the United States. In particular, in North America, the Tiphiid vernalise wasp has been exploited, which would seem easy to adapt even in our territory. The small wasp (only 10 mm long) has Asian origins and uses the larvae of the popillia japonica as a nest for laying its eggs.

Another antagonist is the already known Bacillus Thuringiensis, a bacterium that can already be purchased in formulas. I have already mentioned it in the past because it is the same bacterium used in the biological fight against the boxwood borer. Also, with the fight through the Bacillus Thuringiensis you go to attack the popillia japonica in the larval stage of its biological cycle. In order to start the biological control of popillia japonica on its own, it is possible to buy water-dispersible granules from Amazon that allow the Bacillus Thuringiensis bacterium to penetrate the soil and eliminate papillia japonica larvae.

Thrips

Thrips are parasites - or pests - of plants and represent one of the most annoying and difficult problems to solve in indoor cultivation. Therefore, it is advisable to prevent possible infestations. In this article we will talk about how to prevent and eliminate thrips with natural methods (biological control) or traditional insecticides (chemical control).

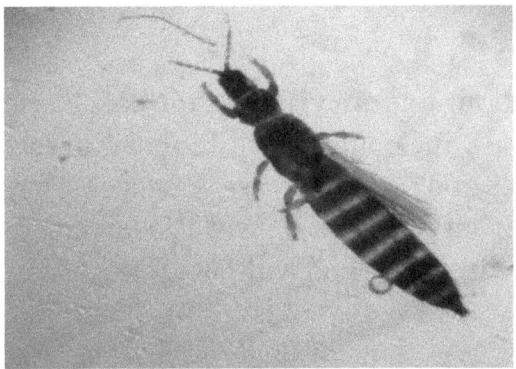

But first let's see what they are and how they behave.

Like many other types of parasites, they also attach themselves to the structure of the plant, in particular to the leaves, and suck the sap out. These small insects represent one of the biggest problems of all growers, especially those involved in greenhouse and indoor cultivation, also because they reproduce up to 12 times a year and - once they reach adulthood - begin to fly and can, therefore, pass quickly from one plant to another.

Among the plants most attacked by thrips are hemp and cotton plants, but - in reality - they also find other types and varieties of plants attractive. Their ideal climate - to spread and reproduce - is the warm one, so it will be advisable to watch over the plants especially in the summer season.

Thrips are not common unlike other pests, but - in certain greenhouse conditions - these animals can be very aggressive.

Thrips attack the leaves and are usually visible on top of the leaf. In winter, they hibernate and activate at temperatures above 16°C. In indoor cultivation, the artificial climate allows them to be active all year round. The eggs are first found under the leaves and then fall on the ground, and then hatch when temperatures are optimal (26°C to 28°C).

The thrips are about 1,5 mm long and are visible to the naked eye. The adult specimens develop wings but rarely use them, in fact they prefer to walk on the legs and fly only in case of danger. They have a dark colour ranging from yellow to brown. The larvae are half the size of adults, lighter in colour and without wings.

Thrips damage

The thrips cut the leaves - through a structure associated with a tool such as a saw - to drill and scrape the leaves until they reach the sap on which they feed. On the surface of the leaves they leave irregular white or silvery patches, the leaf appears scarred and covered with white crusts. The thrips leave behind them black spots of excrement above and below the leaves. The damage caused by thrips initially resembles that of mites or leaf miners, but in more serious cases they cause the plant to lose its colour.

Thrips are parasites that attack numerous types of plants; among the most frequently damaged are tomato plants, vines, orchids, fruit trees, especially citrus and peach trees. The stings of these annoying animals suck the nutritive elements of the plants they attack and cause widespread depigmentation, which results in abnormal white spots on the leaves, thus causing a state of disease and suffering of the plant. This, in fact, facilitates the arrival and spread of infections due mainly to attacks of alternaria and botrytis, which mainly involve leaves and fruits.

Prevent Tripids

As for all the other types of parasites, also for thrips is the same advice as always, which we have seen in other posts of this blog dedicated to the fight against the most feared parasites: to avoid their spread we need to be careful often and avoid that they colonize our plants. To do so, it is advisable to keep the cultivation environment clean, especially when growing indoors, remove dead leaves and disinfect environments and equipment for daily use, to avoid the proliferation of pests and insects, but also mould and other dangerous organisms.

To prevent an infestation of thrips, it is possible to use yellow and blue chromotropic traps, very similar - in mechanism and functioning - to fly paper, which first attracts flies and then traps them. In outdoor gardens you can also use garlic to keep them away. Another recommendation is to increase protection, using natural products that generate a natural barrier against insects and Neem Oil that nourishes and defends plants in a natural way.

How to fight and eliminate thrips: natural remedies

To eliminate pests, you can introduce natural enemies into the affected area, such as predatory mites. The most effective way to permanently eliminate thrips is to wash the plants with vegetable soap and then use a pyrethrum-based product.

Kevin S. Stevenson
Companion Planting for Beginners

CHAPTER 10 – Planning Your Garden

Companion Plants

The mixed-crop garden makes us aware of nature's own trends:

- Plants form plant associations from which they mutually benefit.
- No soil remains free of plant cover
- There are never plants in monoculture
- Never find two plants near each other that damage each other
- Natural plant associations are formed on soils that have the composition essential to their prosperity.
- In nature as in a vegetable garden the life of these associations is conditioned by the factors that act above ground but above all by what happens in the radical sphere.

Achillea (achillea millefolium)

Yarrow increases the aromatic qualities of all herbs.

In much smaller proportions, at the edges, yarrow helps most vegetables.

It grows undisturbed even on small flowerbeds and on the passage, because it can be walked on without damage.

Garlic

Garlic promotes the growth of vetch.

Garlic and roses have mutually beneficial effects.

Garlic, onions and shallots inhibit the growth of peas and beans.

European farmers used to put pieces of garlic in the grain to protect it from weevil.

An infusion made with garlic, onion or chives can be used to fight serious diseases such as downy mildew on potatoes and tomatoes. It is also used against the mould of drupes (stone fruits). The infusion should be used within a short time after its preparation.

Asparagus

Asparagus receives aid directly from tomatoes, which they receive in return. In this "vital exchange" we get rid of the work of cleaning the asparagus flowerbed (perennial plant) from weeds several times during the season. After the asparagus harvest in late spring, the soil is ready to receive the tenderest tomato seedlings. Growing them during their long growing season, directly up to the frost, ensures that there will be no weeds in the asparagus bed. But this is only one side of their mutually beneficial relationship. There is a relationship between the two growing plants that ensures their compatibility.

Asparagus also benefits from parsley, which fits perfectly into the pattern of tomato plants.

One of the few insects that give asparagus problems is the asparagus cryocer (asparagus criocerts), which can be kept under control by leaving the hens free to roam around the asparagus plot; but a way should be found to protect the tomatoes, because the hens go crazy for these fruits even when they are green, not yet ripe.

A substance called asparagine has been isolated, which has a good influence on tomatoes, and helps keep some of the insects that attack them away.

Beets

Beets grow well next to dwarf green beans, onions or kohlrabi.

They grow stunted near climbing beans and are damaged by field mustard.

Lettuce and cabbage thrive on beets.

Basil

The aromatic herbs and plants that bloom in summer are good for the garden because they revive and stimulate the sometimes poor and monotonous qualities of some vegetables.

However, it should be noted that basil does not like rue. Perhaps this is a disharmony that the attentive horticulturist should recognize from the intrinsic nature of these two plants: basil is one of the sweetest, as a smell, and rue is certainly the most bitter of all plants.

Borage

Strawberries and borage help each other

If the borage plants are in minimal proportion, it will also be good to reduce the number of strawberry plants.

Some horticulturists, however, prefer to keep the borage out of these flowerbeds, because it is a plant with very wide foliage, and takes up quite a lot of space.

The bees show evident enthusiasm for borage in bloom.

Chamomile

In peppermint crops, small quantities of chamomile plants increase their content in essential oils. But by increasing the proportion of chamomile, the amount of oil in the mint decreases. This information has been controlled in many experimental plots, in various combinations.

Chamomile in the wheat field in the ratio of one plant for every 100 wheat helps the wheat to ripen fuller and heavier ears. But if chamomile is more widespread it inhibits the growth of neighbouring plants and the wheat gives small, light seeds.

Chamomile also helps neighbouring onions, but only if the proportion is of one chamomile plant for every three metres of onions. It is also good when grown with cabbage.

Chamomile tea has good effects against a good number of plant diseases, especially when the plants to be treated are young. It can be used to prevent rotting in greenhouses and seedbeds the best way to prepare the infusion is to soak the dried flowers in cold water for a day or two.

Carrot

When preparing heavy soil for carrot cultivation, it is best to plant flax or soy beans the year before to lighten the soil and make it crumbly.

H. Molisch has made a study of crop associations; he has isolated a substance extracted from carrot roots that has beneficial effects on pea growth. Carrots grow well with lettuce, chives and red radishes.

The carrot fly (Psila rosae) is a terrible scourge of the carrot that gives many problems. The larva of this insect attacks the roots of young plants. It often reaches the pupa stage in ripe and already stored carrots. Various other plants have proven to repel them: onions, leeks and strongly smelling herbs such as rosemary, wormwood and sage. As H. Thiess reports in Lebendige Erde, (May 1963), the rind (S. hispanica) has the ability to repel carrot flies. He used to plant carrots and rind alternately. The latter is sometimes called the oyster plant because of its taste.

An English horticulturist recommends sowing un-thinned carrot seeds, so as to avoid thinning, because he observed that the uprooting of small plants seems to attract the fly. He also recommends sowing two parts of leek seeds and three parts of carrot seeds. The carrots will be ready to harvest soon, giving the leeks time to ripen before autumn. The presence of leeks seems to keep the carrot fly away.

After harvesting, the carrots should not be stored in the cellar near the apples, because the latter give them a bitter taste.

Cabbage

When we talk about the cabbage family, we include cauliflower, broccoli, Brussels sprouts, cabbage and cabbage. A close study of the members of this family reveals that the development of all these plants took place in a uni-directional manner. The cabbage was developed to obtain a single huge terminal bud, to which the flowering process is subordinated. This uni directional evolution results in a life cycle that is affected by any disturbance: it is a plant of rapid decay due to adverse conditions. The cabbage receives great help, therefore, if it is surrounded by plants that have many flowers, or that are strongly aromatic. Both of these characteristics help to compensate for the weaknesses of the cabbage plant.

It is good to soak the roots of the cabbage, at the time of transplanting, in a paste made from cow manure, clay. This is suggested as an aid against cabbage hernia. After transplanting, the cabbage seedlings should be covered with semi-mature compound. If this is done before the soil dries out, it will be of great help during drought.

Cabbage should not be grown in the same place for two years in a row to avoid the danger of cabbage hernia.

Late cabbages and new potatoes grow well together.

They should be planted when they are tamped down for the first time. Cabbages thrive on dill, chamomile, sage, wormwood, rosemary, and generally on plants of the mint family.

Cabbage does not like strawberries, but beets.

One of the insects that most infest cabbages is the cabbage butterfly, which can be kept away with the following plants, grown nearby: tomatoes, sage, rosemary, hyssop, thyme, mint, hemp, wormwood and abrotanum (Artemisia abrotanum).

In an experimental plantation, the tomatoes, placed near the cabbage, kept the cabbage away.

When cauliflower and nettle occupy neighbouring plots, if the cauliflower is planted too thick, it will increase the growth of nettle.

Kohlrabi

The kohlrabi, a member of the cabbage family, grows well with beets and onions.

It has harmful effects on tomatoes.

It does not grow well near climbing beans.

Chervil

Chervil is described in books as one of the easiest aromatic herbs to grow. We didn't find it until we learned that it wants partial shade in the summer. It now covers the ground and reseeds itself, with long, delicately cut leaves and a slight aromatic smell.

Chervil and radishes are friendly, mutually beneficial plants, and experimenters report that radishes grown close to chervil have a spicier taste.

It is worth noting that the old botanical name, Chaerophyllum, comes from two Greek words that together mean that the leaves give joy.

Cucumbers

Cucumbers appreciate a little shade. They grow well in alternating rows of maize fields. They also grow well in alternating rows with new potatoes and early cabbage. Some radishes seeds planted at the top of the furrow repel the cucumber beetle.

Bordures around the cucumber plot may contain associated crops of kohlrabi and lettuce, kohlrabi and early cabbage, celeriac, and lettuce or low beans, or lettuce and radishes.

A bean border helps the cucumbers, and they help the beans in return. Cucumbers go well with sunflowers.

Cucumbers get the most benefit from a compound made from horse manure and turf, especially if it contains weed.

If the cucumber plant is attacked by downy mildew, it will appear in the form of yellowish-brown spots, with a reddish-grey mould on the underside. This disease can be prevented by using nettle macerate.

Krasil'nikov cites experiments that show that potatoes grown near cucumbers had a greater tendency to be affected by downy mildew.

Onions

These bulbous plants belong to the liliaceae family together with leeks, garlic, shallots and chives. They grow well with beets. The onions in the garden are supported by chamomile in the proportion of one chamomile plant per 3.5 linear metres of onions.

In very good soil, early lettuce helps the onions, as well as some savory plants.

Alternating rows of onions to rows of carrots serves the dual purpose of repelling both onion and carrot flies.

Onions, garlic and shallots inhibit the growth of peas and beans.

Onion juice is effective against bee and wasp stings.

Companion Crops

There are various reasons why certain combinations of plants are successful. Plants that have complementary physical needs adapt well to each other.

For example, a plant that needs a lot of light can be a good associate of another that can tolerate partial shade. Plants that require a lot of moisture can get along well with others that need less.

Plants with deep roots open the soil for other species with shallower roots. Deep-rooting plants use a different part of the soil than the surface roots.

Similarly, tall plants use a different part of the area above the garden from that occupied by shallow plants.

Plants that require a lot of nutrition should be followed by those that require little, or by plants that enrich the soil again, such as leguminous plants.

Plants that cannot compete with weeds should follow those that leave the soil free of weeds.

Horticulturists and biochemists are still investigating other, less obvious factors in the plant's environment that may affect its health, such as scent, leaf and root exudation, or the root influences of other plants further away.

Interspersed Crops

When several crops are planted in the same space, they are said to be interspersed, and the harvest takes place at different times. After the first crop is harvested, the second one stays on the ground until it is ready to be harvested.

With a crop such as broad beans, it is of great help to plant interspersed spinach that provides shade on the ground and prevents the soil surface from breaking or crushing, which would attract the simulium. Spinach also helps to maintain the microscopic life of the soil and its humidity. Spinach is rich in saponins that are beneficial for crops like cabbage.

Observation of external requirements, and our experience, teach us not to put a plant requiring light next to a tall plant with wide, shady leaves, nor to put a plant in need of moisture together with another plant that has the same moisture requirements.

Apart from their particular nutritional needs, plants are chemically influenced in four recognised ways: 1) by aroma; 2) by exudation of leaves and roots; 3) by the roots of other plants; 4) by soil microorganisms.

Here are some other examples of intercropped crops: peas or dwarf peas, if planted with new potatoes, do not grow well; the proximity of carrots increases their development.

For a long time, Dutch horticulturists have grown leeks and onions together with carrots. Onions also go well with red beets, strawberries and tomatoes. It is said that on good soil a little chamomile tea spread among the onions helps them. Planting beans next to onions is not good practice. Celery is best interspersed with members of the cabbage family, especially cauliflower. Cucumbers like to have other plants grown on the edges, such as beans or corn, which protect them from the wind within a slightly enclosed space. Cucumbers also grow well. between annual 'hedges' of maize rows. Nettle increases the content of essential oils in aromatic herbs.

Plant Combinations to Avoid

Some combinations of plants are definitely to be avoided.

Among the aromatic herbs, rue and basil do not thrive next to each other.

Fennel seems to have the most dubious character: it prevents the germination of cumin and coriander, disturbs the growth of dwarf beans, and inhibits the growth of tomato.

Tomato and kohlrabi do not like to grow together. In fact, most of the cabbage family should not be grown near tomatoes.

The tomato has such a dislike for weed (Agropyron repens) that it can very well be used to suppress it.

Dandelion

The dandelion exhales ethylene gas, which inhibits the height growth of nearby plants. It also causes early flowering and ripening of the fruits of the plants around it.

The dandelion has a special affinity with alfalfa.

Its leaves are highly nutritious: they are rich in vitamin A, iron and mineral salts. The young leaves can be served as a salad or cooked like spinach.

As medicinal herb it is suitable for numb livers.

The roots, dried and roasted, are an excellent coffee substitute.

Beans and Green Beans

Beans help celery if planted in the ratio of one beanstalk to six celery.

Beans and cucumbers help each other if the beans are planted around the cucumbers.

Dwarf green beans grow better with cabbage than just beans.

Green beans and fennel have to stay far away, their incompatibility is mutual.

Green beans and strawberries like each other. When the first biodynamic publications were printed in the 1930s, they recorded that strawberries and beans were mutually beneficial. The writings did not state what kind of beans exactly. Several experiments were organised and it became clear that green beans planted on the strawberry plots grew considerably better than those on the control plots; strawberries also benefited appreciably from their proximity to green beans.

Beans and broad beans (Phaseolus e Viciafaba)

Since beans are among the most useful and popular vegetables, and are often found in small vegetable gardens, many possibilities of combining both good and bad have been observed in relation to them.

Beans develop best when alternating with carrots and cauliflowers. They receive help from carrots. They also go well with beets. Beans also help cucumbers and cabbage.

If they are planted together with leeks and root celery in moderate amounts, they create a good combination, but if the beans are planted too thickly between the leeks and celery, all three are hindered.

In general, the beans are choked with onions, garlic and shallots.

In a large maize plantation, broad beans are an excellent combination.

Even in the home-grown vegetable garden, maize and climbing beans grow well together, because this type of bean can be climbed on maize stalks.

In large open field plantations of broad beans and beans, oats also have an affinity with them.

For a border around a small vegetable garden, climbing beans are excellent. They can also be conveniently used as a border for a plot of maize to protect it from excessive wind. The beans enrich the soil with nitrogen, nitrogen which is then absorbed by the maize. Rows of maize can be used as a windbreak for beans; in return they enrich the soil for maize with nitrogen.

Beans and Potatoes

English horticulturists have experimented with this association for many seasons, because the first reference to "broad bean" with potatoes had already been written in 1779 by W. Speechly, who recommended making furrows 90 cm apart, with the potato furrows 45 cm apart. Among the potato plants he transplanted the broad beans and pointed out that the bean plants, being transplanted earlier, were further ahead in the growth of both potatoes and weeds.

It has been customary for many years for American horticulturists to plant green beans, beans or dwarf beans, alternating with potatoes. In some years, insect control has been better than in others, but in general it has been found that potatoes keep away the weevil from the broad beans, while beans sufficiently reduce the activity of the potato's Colorado beetle so that it can be removed with the hands.

Strawberry

In biodynamic farming, strawberry crops have often been accompanied by their favourite associates: beans, lettuce, spinach, and especially borage.

It is reported that many years ago pyrethrum was planted along strawberry plots as a prevention against pests.

They are also found well near a fir tree hedge.

Strawberries do not like cabbage.

Strawberries like the mixture containing pine and straw needles, and also appreciate a covering of pine and fir needles. It is said that the covering of pine needles gives the strawberries the taste of wild strawberries. A special mixture for strawberries can be made with straw, pine needles, a little green material, with the usual intermediate layers of soil, a small amount of lime.

A horticulturist has written to us suggesting to plant legumes and a little border thyme.

Buckwheat

Buckwheat grows on the poorest soils and collects large amounts of calcium which it returns to the soil when it is overgrown.

It also suffocates weeds and over time uproots them, helping to soften heavy soils.

Calcium and the green overgrown plant enrich the soil over time.

Buckwheat enters into antagonism with autumn wheat.

Maize

Sweet maize grows well with new potatoes.

It benefits from beans and peas; these help the soil by enriching it with nitrogen that the maize uses. The beans take advantage of the light shade provided by the maize plants.

Other plants that appreciate the protective shade of maize are melons, pumpkins, courgettes and cucumbers.

On the other hand, the presence of a cucumber border is beneficial for maize.

Rows of maize in windy areas help to break the wind until a good hedge has grown.

It is said that when the first pioneers came to America, they found that Indians were growing maize and pumpkins together; perhaps this is one of the first examples in America of associated crops.

Lettuce

Since lettuce is a favourite vegetable and grows fast, it has been observed for many years, and many things are known about its preferences for plants to be associated with it.

For example: Lettuce loves strawberries, is helped by the presence of carrots, and makes radishes tender in summer.

Lettuce prefers partial shade in summer.

Spring lettuce, in very good soil, helps the onions.

Biodynamic literature speaks of lucky combinations of lettuce, cabbage and beets grown together.

Lupin

The first one (L. luteus) is the bitter one that makes yellow flowers, the L. polyphyllus is very tall with blue flowers.

Both lupines, bitter and sweet, are used to reclaim sandy soils.

Lupines leave behind a better and more crumbly soil (see also under Legumes, about nature's use of lupines in the re-vegetation of volcanic ash in Alaska).

Eggplant

To protect the eggplant from the potato Dorifora (Colorado beetle), it is best to plant it among the green beans.

The potato dorifora also prefer aubergines to potatoes, but green beans repel these insects from the grooves of aubergines and potatoes.

An eggplant border around the potato plot will concentrate the dorifora where they can be picked up and kept under control.

Nettle

Nettle has at least three properties that illustrate its dynamic character:

1) It helps neighbouring plants to grow more resistant to rotting
2) It modifies chemical processes in neighbouring plants. F. Lippert, who treated the medicinal herb garden of a pharmaceutical industry, reports that nettle grown in association with other plants increased the essential oil content up to 20% in valerian, more than 80% in arcangelica, 10-20% in marjoram, 10% in sage, and 10% in peppermint.
3) Stimulates the formation of humus.

This third property can be studied if you dig with the shovel the soil near the roots of a nettle and observe the type of humus that has formed: a dark blackish neutral humus. The leaves and stalk of this plant rot until it becomes an ideal humus. There may also be secretions on the roots that stimulate life and fermentation.

Nettle has very fine hairs on its leaves and stem, which contain formic acid, and perhaps a still unknown poison (which can be neutralized by rubbing green parts of balsamin or any species of the sorrel family, including rhubarb) on the skin.

Very young plants cooked like spinach in early spring are an excellent table vegetable. Chicks devour chopped nettle with greed and these leaves are nutritious and suitable for preventing coccidiosis and diarrhoea in poultry.

Nettle is rich in vitamins and iron, something known since ancient times, when it was used as a remedy against anaemia and to give vitality to those who ate it.

To make the fermented extract, which is used as a liquid green fertilizer, cover the cut grass with water and let it decompose for three weeks. The nettle plants will be completely undone. During the three weeks and afterwards, this nettle liquid will promote the development of the plants and protect them against adverse conditions. It should be sprayed on the plants to strengthen them, to help them overcome drought, etc.

Potatoes

We know that new potatoes grow well with beans, maize, cabbage and peas: you plant two rows of peas alternating with two of new potatoes. The potatoes like the nitrogen provided by the pea roots.

Potatoes and English broad beans are good with it. Broad beans need air and have a better development if they are planted in a maximum of three rows in a row. Potatoes, when they follow a rye crop, grow particularly well.

A small amount of horseradish, a plant in every corner of the potato plot, contributes to the general health of the potato plants. Lamio, sainfoin and nasturtium, according to old New England traditions, are good for nearby potatoes.

If hemp grows near potatoes, it is unlikely that they will be attacked by downy mildew, the cause of brown rot. It has also been observed by some scientists that the resistance of potatoes to brown rot is lower in the vicinity of sunflowers, tomatoes, apple trees, cherry trees, raspberries, pumpkins and cucumbers. Potatoes grown near a birch forest rot more easily than potatoes grown near pine trees.

Potatoes and sunflowers get in each other's way.

The secretions of potato roots somehow inhibit the development of tomatoes.

Potatoes should not be grown close to the saltbush, because this inhibits their development. The saltbush (Atriplex hortensis) is related to chenopodium. It thrives well near potatoes, but if it spreads too much, it indicates that the soil in the potato field is depleted.

It is advisable to plant new potatoes in the garden, and after the first tamping with the hoe, plant cabbage among the potatoes.

The cabbage should then thrive.

If the potatoes develop a lot of leaves, they suppress a lot of weeds. If the soil is infested with meal, it is a sign that the potatoes have been grown too long, and it is time to change crops.

Rows of potatoes alternating with beans repel epylachna. Rows of green beans (but not Lima beans) alternating with rows of potatoes will keep the potato's dorifora away.

Flax planted between the rows of potatoes will greatly reduce the number of weeds. Research is underway to determine the relationship between marigold and eel, a nematode, of the potato. There is also evidence that clovers brought to the United States from Ireland in 1964 had to be quarantined in order to avoid the import of the golden nematode, "a small harmful vermiform insect that seriously damages potatoes and tomatoes, but which does no harm to clovers, exploited only to have a passage attached to their roots".

The Dorifora prefer aubergines to potatoes. An aubergine border around a potato plot gives you the chance to gather, catch and destroy most of the doryphores.

Peas

The peas love radishes, carrots, cucumbers, corn, beans and turnips.

The growth of peas is inhibited by onions, garlic and shallots.

Normally, peas are never grown on the same soil for two years.

Some say that peas do not thrive near new potatoes, but most horticulturists report that peas and potatoes are a good combination, alternating 2 rows of peas with two rows of new potatoes.

Potatoes like the nitrogen provided by the pea roots.

Tomato

Tomatoes and asparagus help each other.

Parsley goes well with both.

Tomatoes help the early cabbage. Tomatoes and all varieties of brassica, grown together, help repel the cabbage butterfly.

The tomato emits root secretions that have an inhibitory effect on young apricot saplings.

It is also proven that potatoes, grown close to tomatoes, had no resistance to downy mildew.

In 1950 Porozhikov noted that certain volatile substances emitted by tomatoes had an inhibitory effect on certain insects that attacked currant bushes. According to the observations of this author, currant bushes planted near tomatoes are not infested by these insects.

Tomatoes like to grow in the same place year after year and prefer a compound made with tomato stalks and leaves.

They do not grow well in the vicinity of kohlrabi and fennel.

Tomatoes get help from nettle. The presence of nettle in the surroundings makes the tomatoes keep better, with little risk of mould or rotting.

Leeks

Leeks (also onions) and celery grow well together, sown in alternating furrows.

Composted pork manure is the best for leeks and celery.

Leeks thrive well in alternating rows with celeriac. The slender leek grows well among the celeriac leaves: both love potassium and goat and pig manure.

The leek benefits from carrots, and in return helps them repel the carrot fly.

Parsley

Parsley helps roses that are close by and is useful for tomatoes.

Parsley in bloom in the garden is particularly popular with bees. There are five species in the genus, all native to the old world.

Oak

The oak tree is protective of other trees and helps them: citrus fruits are among them.

The cover made of oak leaves or bark repels slugs, the agrotide, and phyllophagous larvae. It is spread on the paths of the vegetable garden and along the seedbeds, between the rows.

The oak has the property of accumulating an incredible amount of calcium in the bark during growth. The highest calcium content in the ashes was found in oaks that lived on sandy, calcium-deficient soil.

Radishes

All the radishes, both black and white, help the other vegetables in the garden.

Peas and radishes help each other.

If the radishes are planted near the nasturtiums, they are helped and taste perfect.

The leaf lettuce makes the radishes softer in summer.

Chervil and radishes in alternating furrows are helpful to each other, and chervil gives the radishes a spicy taste.

Climbing beans love radishes.

Some radishes seeds buried near cucumber plants or other plants with shoots help to fight the cucumber beetle (Diabrotica dictata).

Radishes and hyssop do not like each other.

Roses

Roses and garlic are mutually beneficial, as has been proven by countless rose growers in recent years.

From Europe we learn that Bulgarian gardeners grow onions and garlic interspersed with roses, resulting in an intensified scent and increased production. This is one of the great mysteries of associated crops.

It is even useful to fertilize rose bushes with garlic and onion waste. Onions also repel the insects in the roses.

Roses are also helped by the presence of parsley in the vicinity.

Reseda is another plant that roses like. It forms a low soil cover, is a border plant for rose beds and at the same time helps them.

Another plant that roses like is lupine, especially perennial lupine, which helps to increase the nitrogen in the soil and attract earthworms.

A plant that the rose does not like is boxwood: it has widespread woody roots that interfere with the roots of rose bushes.

It is better to place roses close to plants whose roots are deep rather than extensive.

Celery

Like celeriac, celery benefits from leeks, grown close together and in alternating rows.

Both plants love compost pig manure.

Both celery and leeks grow well in furrows.

Tomatoes are also good neighbours of celery.

Another good companion is the dwarf bean. For many years biodynamic farmers have followed the practice of planting one dwarf bean for every six celery plants.

In 1951 a research was conducted in Germany that included data on the protective effects of celery. The results were concentrated in the statement that 'when the cabbage grows close to this plant it is less affected by microorganisms'. This is just one example among many with which modern science has confirmed the oral traditions of previous generations.

Celeriac

Celeriac is a variety of celeriac that develops a large edible root that should be known: more appreciated in America. The taste is like celery, but it is quite easier to grow.

It has been recognized that hairy vetch prepares the ground for celeriac. Vetch should be sown early and allowed to grow until late spring. When the weather is warm enough to sow celery, the vetches should be cut and the green part put into the mixture. The soil should be spat or ploughed and lightly covered with mature manure; then the celeriac should be sown.

This plant needs a rich and crumbly soil with a lot of potassium.

The leek is also a leek lover of potassium, and is a good substitute for celeriac. In such a combination, the celery plants should be at a distance of 30-40 cm, and the leeks 20-30 cm in the next furrow, with alternating furrows. Both need the whole season to ripen, and continue to grow even in the cool autumn climate. The leeks can be left in the ground all winter long, but they will rot or form seeds by the beginning of the following spring.

American beans (Phaseolus coccineus) grown in grooves next to celeriac beans have resulted in better celeriac production than the nearby experimental plot where there were no beans.

The edible part of this plant, a large bulbous root, can be cut into slices or pieces for salads or soups. This bulbous root is complementary to the thin, long leek stem when the two plants grow together in the biodynamic garden; it is easier to grow than celery because it does not require burying.

Marigold

In the public parks of a city in the Netherlands, instead of using spray products or chemical soil disinfectants to get rid of the little nematode worm that infested the soil in the rose beds, the Plant Protection Service decided to try using marigold (imported from Mexico).

The plant secretes from its roots a substance that kills soil nematodes. Planted among the roses they destroyed the nematodes, while the rose beds left without marigolds continued to suffer from the infestation. This story is reported by Rachel Carson in Silent Spring; she also adds that in many places, horticulturists and gardeners now know how to plant marigolds to fight nematodes in other crops.

A friend writes from Ohio that he visited a vegetable garden where gardeners had long made a habit of growing marigolds among tomato plants: tomatoes grow better and bear more fruit with marigolds than without them.

The marigold has been successfully used to fight potato nematodes.

It is also a cure against tomato whitefly, and is used in greenhouses. The smell of marigold leaves and old marigold flowers has the effect of repelling insects.

Marigold has been successfully used to repel the weevil of the broad beans.

Valerian

Edging helps most vegetables.

It is a phosphorus specialist, i.e. it stimulates phosphorus activity in its vicinity.

Valerian attracts earthworms. It also attracts cats, if its roots are crushed and therefore give off their smell).

The positive influence of valerian can be enhanced by making a spray product with its juice. It has been written that "it is a particular joy for earthworms that are attracted to it".

Valerian should be sprayed once a month in summer because it increases the general health of the plants and their resistance. It can be sprayed on the soil, and on all plants, at whatever stage of growth they are, unlike other spraying products, which require certain precautions.

Pumpkins

Pumpkins and corn are good neighbours.

On the contrary, pumpkins don't want to be near potatoes.

Kevin S. Stevenson
Companion Planting for Beginners

CHAPTER 11 - How to create the Compost

Reducing waste is an urgent necessity in our consumer society. The high costs associated with waste and the pollution produced by disposal and recovery operations require it.

Every year, the average citizen contributes 80 kg of organic waste to separate waste collection. This rises to 100 if we also consider biodegradable waste such as wood, paper and textiles. This considerable amount of waste could be reduced if each of us were to transform compost into natural fertiliser on our own, instead of recycling it.

An environmentally friendly, cost-effective choice. It would also mean less use of chemical fertilisers.

Compost is what remains after you have started a domestic composting process. That is, the process of decomposition and humification on residues of organic substances, such as leaves in your garden, grass cut from the lawn etc.

Depending on the composting method you have adopted you will get a different type of compost but basically you can categorize them into 3 types:

1. fresh compost
2. ready compost
3. mature compost

Fresh compost (2 to 4 months in the case of composting with cumulation) is still being processed. As it is still rich in nutrients, it is excellent as a fertilizer and for plant growth. However, be careful to apply it directly to the roots because this compost is still not very stable.

The ready compost (5 to 8 months), on the other hand, is stable, as the decomposition process no longer produces heat. On the other hand, it is less suitable for use as a fertiliser. We recommend using it in vegetable gardens or gardens as a fertiliser before sowing or transplanting.

Mature compost (12/18 or 24 months) is the most stable compost. Therefore, it is the least suitable as a fertilizer. However, it is perfect in direct contact with roots or seeds and as soil for potted plants or even in the case of reseeding lawns.

Now let's see how to obtain it with a simple process of understanding and execution.

How to make Compost

We said that by compost we mean the product of the accelerated, man-made, controlled decomposition of organic substances. Among them, kitchen waste. Mainly remnants of vegetables, fruit peels, coffee and tea grounds, egg shells, fireplace ashes, etc.

But also gardening. For example, pruning branches, mowing lawns, dried leaves, withered flowers, garden waste.

Domestic composting can be carried out by purchasing composting equipment that is not excessively expensive. Those for internal use range from 50 to 100 euros, the others for external use from 200 to 300 euros, being also equipped with temperature control and automatic stirring.

The advantages of compost

Domestic composting offers a number of advantages.

First of all, it guarantees the correct closure of the waste cycle, as the workforce makes up about one third of the total household garbage. DIY compost avoids landfill or incineration, thus reducing disposal costs. At the end of the domestic composting procedure, then, we will have a natural organic fertiliser available.

This will be used in the garden, in the garden or for potted plants instead of polluting chemical fertilisers. We will thus save money by limiting the purchase of soil, substrates and organic fertilisers. And at the same time, we will reduce the air pollution produced by the combustion of this waste, avoiding leachate infiltration into the soil.

Compost, as a natural organic fertilizer, gradually releases into the soil the elements essential for the development of plants, such as nitrogen, phosphorus, potassium and trace elements.

What can and cannot become compost

If you want to compost at home, you must first pay attention to what you put in the composter.

The kitchen and gardening waste mentioned above, as well as other biodegradable materials, are fine. These include uncoated paper, cardboard, sawdust and shavings from untreated wood.

Please note that all glass, plastic and metal objects, synthetic fabrics, chemicals, expired medicines, coated paper and cat and dog litter must be avoided.

With great caution, leftovers of food of animal origin and food cooked in small quantities can also be added. Same warning for leaves of plants resistant to degradation (magnolia, beech, chestnut, conifer needles etc.).

How to make compost: composting in piles

We now come to the various forms of composting. The most widespread is certainly the cumulation. Here we will have to choose places that can be used all year round, that can be irrigated and that are in the shade of trees that lose their leaves in winter. In winter we must allow solar radiation, while in summer the sunlight must be mitigated. Putting chopped wood under the heap (10-15 cm) is another good practice to avoid the formation of mud during the winter months.

The minimum height of the pile must be 50-60 cm in order to retain heat and ensure microbial activity. However, the height must not exceed 1.3-1.5 metres, otherwise the material may compact under its weight.

The best shape in summer is the trapeze shape. It absorbs rain adequately and replaces evaporated water. In winter, on the contrary, it is good practice to use the triangular shape, to avoid the excessive accumulation of rain inside the heap, given the lower evaporation.

The secrets to making good compost

The secret to successful composting lies in the correct mixing of the waste. This activity is fundamental to allow the right activity of microorganisms and avoid the onset of putrefaction phenomena, with the consequent bad odours.

In practice, a correct stratification must be carried out, alternating the most humid and nitrogenous waste (grass clippings and kitchen residues) with the driest and most carbonic waste (shredded branches, broken cardboard, wood shavings, dry leaves, straw, etc.), which guarantee good porosity and the correct supply of oxygen to the heap. The initial water content must be between 45 and 65%, while as far as the right nitrogen-carbon ratio is concerned, it is good to know that for every gram of the first one you need 20 or 30 of the second one.

To ensure the correct moisture supply, the heap can be covered during rainy periods with materials such as "non-woven fabric" or jute sheets or 5-10 cm layers of leaves and straw. In this way we can retain the water without compromising the air circulation. The cover can also be useful to protect against excessive drying during the summer months.

Another aspect not to be underestimated for the success of composting is the right oxygenation. It is essential for bacteria that operate biodegradation in aerobic conditions. For a correct exchange of air, it is therefore necessary not to compress the material of the pile and turn it periodically with a fork, an operation to be repeated frequently if the pile is not very porous.

How to make the compost: the concimaia

An alternative to the heap can be the manure plant. It consists of a hole dug into the ground where organic waste is stored. In this case, however, there may be problems with the tendency to accumulate too much water, especially in the case of a waterproofed bottom.

Another typical problem is the insufficient exchange of oxygen with the outside by the materials deposited on the bottom.

Those who choose this system will therefore have to take certain measures. These include the insertion of drainage pipes, a layer of gravel or a pallet under the organic material placed in the hole.

The same pallets can also be used to separate the waste from the wall of the hole, in order to ensure a good exchange of air.

How to compost using the composter

As you can guess, the mound is particularly suitable for those who live in houses with large gardens that produce large quantities of branches and green waste. Composters made of plastic, wood or net, on the other hand, are more useful for those citizens who have small and medium sized gardens that produce less waste.

They are containers of variable volumes (from 200 to 1,000 litres), with openings of various types. Their use makes it possible to limit the visual impact of decaying materials, guaranteeing their sanitation and being less affected by atmospheric conditions. However, there may be difficulties in turning the material, if they cannot be opened on one side. If you are planning to purchase a plastic composter, you prefer those that have systems in the interior walls that promote air circulation.

The operation of these instruments is very simple. After the separate collection, all you have to do is insert a layer of coarse branches at its base, then alternatively adding layers of nitrogen and carbon waste, according to the same principle analysed above. After 3-4 months, the vegetable waste must be turned over and then reinserted into the composter.

After a period of 5-6 months, the lower part of the waste, brown in colour and similar to the humus of the undergrowth, will have produced a homogeneous compost already available for use. This fraction will then have to be sieved and left to dry in the sun for a few days. Wood waste not yet processed must instead be reintroduced into the composter.

Of course, the use of these do-it-yourself tools implies the same good practice as for the pile. First and foremost, it is necessary to ensure proper mixing by alternating nitrogen and carbon layers. Then it is necessary to ensure good air circulation by inserting coarse branches and turning the material once every 6 months. Finally, it is necessary to maintain optimal humidity (55-60%), which favours the reproduction of aerobic microorganisms.

Generally, the compost is ready after about 12-20 weeks in winter and 10-15 weeks in summer. The completion of its degradation is evident both from the appearance and the characteristic smell.

A DIY composter

There is also the possibility of building your own composter. All you need to do is buy three metres of 2.5 x 5 cm galvanised wire mesh, one metre high, and then build a cylinder stopped in two places with wire or "S" shaped hooks. The latter must be externally covered with jute fabric 70 cm high, always fixed with iron wire or "S" shaped hooks and finally covered with a waterproof fabric.

Your compost can be used as a fertiliser and fertilizer for the reseeding of degraded turf, as a partial or even total substitute for peaty soil, as organic fertilizer and as plant nutrition.

Odorless Compost with Japanese fermentation

Let's close with a curiosity, which may become important in the future. A Japanese researcher has produced a mixture of bacteria that can increase crop yields in a natural way that could help prevent hunger in the world.

It is called EM (Effective Microorganisms). It is a mixture of bacteria and other microorganisms that can increase the breakdown of food and agricultural residues. This is a particular type of compost that has existed in Japan for hundreds of years, called bokashi.

Unlike common compost, EM is an odourless compost that can therefore be developed in small rooms, even in an apartment. Not only that, it can also process meat or dairy products, which are normally excluded from "classic" systems.

Made for Japanese gardens and farms, EM can integrate bacteria and microorganisms from all over the world.

What can Japanese fermentation be used for

His goal is ambitious. It was developed to support food production, environmental preservation, medical care and energy supply. In a broad sense, its ultimate goal is to foster world peace. In fact, its use during some environmental and humanitarian disasters has been positive. In fact, it has restored fertility to the rice fields swept by the 2011 tsunami in Sendai, Japan, as well as in Fukushima. It has also helped in the Ugandan refugee camps, both for its fertilizing properties and to eliminate smell.

The basis of EM is brewer's yeast, commonly used in the production of beer and bread. It is capable of starting the fermentation process by breaking down complex sugars. The key organisms, however, are microbes that use sunlight to break down organic remains and create nutrients needed to aid plant development. The addition of lactic acid bacteria prevents the proliferation of harmful mushrooms.

There are also more than 80 species of microbes in an EM package. They are all designed for their ability to assimilate waste and turn it into food for ecological agriculture, all in order to have an odourless compost.

Here too we are faced with a technological solution, the result of years of research and experimentation, which works with Nature to solve the problems caused by human beings.

CHAPTER 12 - Crop Rotation

Crop rotation is a cultivation technique whose origins are lost in the mists of time; it is essentially a technique based on alternating, in the same position of the field or garden, after a certain period of time, the cultivation of a given plant with another. The duration of this period can vary; in fact, crop rotation can be two, three or four years; the most commonly used is probably the latter.

Crop rotation has a specific purpose, i.e. to maintain and/or improve the fertility of the soil used for cultivation; this ensures a better productivity of the soil in question.

When replacing plants, the choices are not random, in fact a certain plant must be replaced by another plant belonging to a totally different botanical family so that the greatest benefits can be obtained and the continuity of the production cycle can be kept constant.

Soil Tiredness

Incorrect crop rotation can lead to soil fatigue. The phenomenon of soil fatigue has been studied at an agronomic level for centuries. It starts from the assumption that all cultivated plants do not like to repeat themselves.

The first consequence of this tiredness is a decrease in soil productivity itself. This problem, as said, is compensated for in conventional agriculture by resorting to chemistry.

But operating in monoculture or mono-succession, i.e. repeating the same crop several times in the same piece of land, causes problems on several levels.

For example, there is the continuous uptake by plants of the same nutrients. This does not allow the soil itself to find a balance and therefore depletes it of organic matter.

Furthermore, monoculture always uses the same soil layers, regardless of the type of soil on which it is planted. This is because the root systems that explore the earth are, of course, always the same.

Another direct consequence of the lack of crop rotation is the proliferation of parasite agents, both animal and vegetable. These multiply much faster by repeating the same crop. A glaring example can be that of a parasite such as the potato dorifora, a very harmful insect that is difficult to eradicate. If one year we grow potatoes, therefore, and we have an attack of slight intensity of dorifora, if on that same plot of land the following year we repeat the same cultivation (or we grow a plant of the same family, for example the eggplant), we can be sure that the invasion of the dorifora will worsen.

Another problem of poor or no crop rotation is the increasing difficulty in controlling weeds. Weeds are becoming increasingly specific to the crop and more resistant. Sometimes even good mulching is not enough to control their proliferation.

Finally, wrong crop rotations and repeating the same crops on the same soil can lead to the accumulation of substances that plants secrete naturally. At high concentrations, some of these substances, such as nitrates, can become toxic.

The importance of crop rotation

Cultivation on the same soil of the same crops causes several drawbacks among which we can mention the reduction in the level of soil fertility, the appearance of parasitic diseases, the development of weeds, etc.

Many diseases that attack plants are caused by pathogens, phytophages, parasites, etc. These agents, under certain conditions, can attack a particular family of plants (an example is the so-called downy mildew, a disease that attacks Cucurbitaceae, such as zucchini, pumpkins, watermelons, and Cruciferae, such as cabbage, cauliflowers and broccoli) and feeding on them can survive and reproduce creating significant problems at the production level.

Since the various agents do not attack all plants indiscriminately, the solution for their elimination is to vary the type of crop. By acting in this way, the survival and proliferation of certain pathogens is limited; in fact, crop rotation is a kind of preventive strategy that sometimes also has therapeutic purposes.

With crop rotation it is possible to limit the use of chemical products with a phytosanitary action such as pesticides, pesticides, herbicides, etc.; this limitation allows both an economic saving and to limit the possible problems that their use could cause (many phytosanitary products are dangerous substances that must be handled with great caution).

Thanks to crop rotation, the soil absorbs certain types of nutrients that had been absorbed by the plants previously present; this is particularly useful for the maximization of the crop variety, not to mention that the weed cycle is interrupted.

It has also been noted that crop rotation contributes significantly to improving the physical characteristics of the soil, making it more stable, less degraded, less erodible by weathering and also contributing to more efficient management of infiltrated water resources.

Various crop rotation systems

There are different ways to rotate crops; one of the most used and recommended for amateur gardens is based on the nutritional needs of vegetables. The latter are divided into three macro groups.

The first large group includes all those vegetables that are significant consumers of nutrients:

- cabbage (all types except kohlrabi)
- cucumbers
- salads
- aubergines
- melons
- potatoes
- peppers
- tomatoes
- celeriac and celeriac
- spinach
- pumpkins and zucchini.

In the second group we find all those plants considered to be average consumers of nutrients:

- garlic

- red beards
- chards
- kohlrabi
- carrots
- chicory
- onions
- herbs
- fennel
- warts
- radicchio
- radishes
- rocket
- scorzonera

The third group includes all those vegetables that are considered to be weak consumers of nutrients, that is:

- beans and green beans
- broad beans
- peas
- parsley.

This system of crop rotation involves dividing the area of the garden into three sectors (sectors 1, 2 and 3). Let us supposed to start the cultivation of the vegetable garden: in sector 1 the vegetables of the first group (strong consumers) will be cultivated, in sector 2 the vegetables belonging to the group of medium consumers and in sector 3 the vegetables of the third type will be cultivated.

In the following cycle, in the second sector, the vegetables of the second group will be sown, which will be able to exploit residual fertility, followed by those of the third group, the less demanding ones (most of which belong to the Leguminosae family), which will allow atmospheric nitrogen to be fixed there, thus enriching the soil with useful organic substances and making it suitable for the subsequent cultivation of the plants of the first group, the most demanding ones.

Another crop rotation system involves dividing vegetables into four groups:

- fruit vegetables
- leafy vegetables
- root vegetables
- Flower vegetables.

Watermelons, cucumbers, beans and green beans, broad beans, aubergines, melons, peppers, tomatoes, pumpkins and zucchini belong to the first group.

The second group includes cabbage, chicory, fennel, salads, radicchio, rocket, celery and spinach.

In the third group we find garlic, red beards, carrots, onions, potatoes, leeks, radishes, turnips, scorzonera and celeriac.

In the fourth group there are cauliflowers and aromatic plants.

In the first year the fruit vegetables will be grown, in the second year the flowering vegetables, in the third year the leafy vegetables will be grown and in the last year the root vegetables.

Another system, that of the four-year rotation, provides for the subdivision of the land into four sectors (1, 2, 3, 4).

Example of a four-year rotation in a 100 m2 vegetable garden with a set-aside part

That's how it goes in the first year:

- Sector 1: potatoes
- sector 2: legumes and cabbages
- sector 3: root vegetables
- sector 4: leafy vegetables.

Second year:

- sector 1: leafy vegetables
- sector 2: root vegetables
- sector 3: legumes and cabbages
- sector 4: potatoes.

Third year:

- sector 1: legumes and cabbages

- sector 2: leafy vegetables
- sector 3: potatoes
- sector 4: root vegetables.

Fourth year:

- sector 1: root vegetables
- sector 2: potatoes
- sector 3: leafy vegetables
- sector 4: legumes and cabbages.

When the rotation is finished, the soil will be fertilized and the cycle can begin again.

Alternations According to Botanical Families

An absolute rule is that crops from the same family should not be repeated in succession. Then there is the fact that there are conflicts between some different families.

Let us see some examples with the main crops spread in home gardens.

Chenopodiaceae

Let's start with the Chenopodiaceae, a family to which chard and spinach belong. The rule is that they never repeat themselves, not even in alternation with each other.

Composite

Then we have the Composites, first of all the artichoke, a multi-year plant, which, after its cycle, must not return to the same ground for at least 5 years.

In this same family we have endive, lettuce and radicchio. Given their high diffusion, it is easy to fall into error, but also, they follow the general rule of not repeating themselves and each other. A good succession is with spinach and leeks.

Cruciferous

The Cruciferae, on the other hand, are a large family that includes several species grown in vegetable gardens. Among the best-known vegetables, we have cauliflower, broccoli, kale, cabbage, cabbage, kohlrabi. These are all plants that consume the soil in a significant way. In their crop rotation they must not follow themselves and must also avoid plants of the Solanaceae and Umbelliferae family. Other Cruciferae are radish and rocket which, although they do not use the soil much, should not follow themselves. This caution allows, for example, to avoid the problems with the halos.

A good alternative to these plants is the one with peas or cereals.

Cucurbitaceae

Then we see the Cucurbitaceae, that is watermelon, cucumber, cucumber, melon, pumpkin, zucchini. For the cultivation rotations of this family it is important not to repeat, for at least two years in a row, the cultivations in the same soil, not even inverting them among them. Many people advise to avoid also the succession with the Solanaceae. Good successions are those with cabbage, legumes, salads, cereals, leeks.

Legumes

Continuing on we have the Leguminosae, that is beans, green beans, broad beans, peas, lentils, chickpeas, lupins, peanuts. These are plants that improve the soil, as they can fix atmospheric nitrogen with their roots. They are good in crop rotation with any other plant, but they must not be repeated among themselves.

Liliacee

Another important family is the Liliaceae. Among the best-known species is the asparagus, which is a multi-year crop. At the end of its cycle, it cannot return to the same soil for 5 years. Asparagus must never be followed by potatoes and carrots. Cereals and strawberries are fine.

In this family we also have garlic, onion and leeks. These last crops should never follow themselves and also avoid potatoes and beets. Tomatoes, cabbage, cucumber and legumes are suitable for rotation.

Umbelliferous

Then let's talk about the Umbrelliferae, that is carrot, fennel, parsley, celery. With these crops, especially in the presence of diseases, the crop rotation requires that they must pass from 3 to 5 years before repeating the cultivation. Moreover, they should not be grown after chard. Without problems with diseases, they are fine in crop rotation before and after most other crops.

Solanaceae

Let's finally see the Solanaceae, that is eggplant, potato, pepper, tomato. These are among the most demanding crops in terms of nutrients and consume a lot of soil. Their crop rotation must never see them in succession with each other or even within the same family. Also avoid Cucurbitaceae and Chenopodiaceae.

Excellent is to follow as crop rotation a leguminous plant or, at the limit, some cruciferous ones.

Soil set-aside and green manure

When crop rotations are not respected, we may be faced with soil fatigue. In such cases, a set-aside period should also be considered.

It is not a bad thing for the soil to rest; on the contrary, you can take advantage of the break to fertilise it properly. A period of rest can be considered to be at least six months.

During a rest period you can also opt for green (or green manure) fertilisation. Leguminous plants such as clover or vetch, for example, are the most suitable for this crop.

Leguminous green manure

In general, we say that leguminous green manure is an agricultural practice used in organic production. This practice allows, through sowing and burial of a non-harvesting herbaceous crop, to produce improvements in the soil.

The specific objective of leguminous green manure is natural fertilisation through nitrogen fixation. That is to say, so-called green fertilisation. At the same time, this technique makes it possible to improve the physical structure of the soil by adding organic matter.

As we have seen, the family of leguminous plants is very large and there are several species that can be used. Depending on the species you choose we will have different amounts of nitrogen that will be fixed and biomass (organic matter) that will be supplied. Much used is, for example, the species of the field bean, Vicia faba minor, which can fix more than 150 kg. of nitrogen per hectare of land.

The field bean green manure

The sowing of the green manure comb is usually done at the beginning of autumn. It has a cultivation cycle lasting from 28 to 32 weeks. The green manure, i.e. the burial of the crop, will then take place in spring.

The sowing of the field beans must be intense, we must consider planting about 40-60 plants for one square meter of land. The seed is smaller than the classic field bean, 1000 field bean seeds weigh about 700 g, so do your calculations to understand the amount of seed needed.

In spring, when the green manure period has arrived, that is when the plant is at the end of its cycle, it will be necessary to bury the crop, using the tiller (if you have a tractor) or even a simple motorhoe, burying the organic mass at least 15 cm. deep.

After a further period of rest, about 15-20 days, you will have your soil ready for spring and summer crops. These crops (such as tomatoes, for example) need a lot of nitrogen and organic matter in the soil.

The green manure of legumes, field beans, etc., is very important, especially if you do not have manure or organic compost for natural fertilization. This practice should be repeated every two or three years. This, of course, depends essentially on the condition of the most precious resource we have in our hands: the earth!

Crop rotations in the home garden

This is a problem that every horticulturist is faced with, but which becomes more acute if space is limited.

An idea for efficient planning is to divide the plot of land into several parts (usually at least 4) and draw it according to the crop rotation rules seen above. It is always better to keep one of the parts at rest. Another important shrewdness is to write everything down, keeping a sort of country notebook. If for the first years you can also work from memory, with time it is good to have a written reference.

The division can occur through the creation of flowerbeds, but also only ideally, with hypothetical divisions.

In this way, even those who have a small plot of land can follow a valid crop rotation scheme. And in doing so, healthy and luxuriant productions will be guaranteed, greatly limiting the problems linked to diseases and parasites and the disappointments that come from intensive and repeated cultivation.

CHAPTER 13 - Home for Useful Insects

Surely you have heard of bat houses to install on the balcony or in the garden: a useful way to protect yourself from mosquitoes in summer. In fact, bats are a very natural "mosquito repellent": building a little house where they can find shelter is a way to try to welcome them to kill mosquitoes.

The same happens for other small houses, such as those of insects: from pollinators to predators of parasites, having them as guests in your garden or on the terrace can solve several problems. Knowing that almost all harmful insects have natural predators, you can try to establish a precise balance between prey and predators, hosting "good" insects in a house made especially for them! For example, ladybugs and beetles can hunt down harmful scale insects and aphids: you will have disease-free roses and fruit plants. With bees, bumblebees and butterflies, on the other hand, you can have lush flowers and fruit. Of course, it doesn't make any difference to the insects whether or not you have this little house - you'll have the advantage, as you can take advantage of their beneficial function! By attracting useful insects to your garden or vegetable garden, you can avoid the use of insecticides and synthetic chemicals and always have a healthy, green garden and vegetable garden. For a truly organic and healthy green space that will also help the environment!

How to make the insect-home

You can build your own bug house. That's what you need:

Materials:

- a wooden box
- bamboo reeds (to attract bees)
- sandpaper
- zip
- fastener
- natural materials: grass, twigs, dry leaves, straw, moss (straw and twigs attract ladybugs).

Tools:

- drill
- jigsaw
- hot glue.

Get yourself a wooden box: preferably in raw wood, so as not to damage your guests. An example could be the box containing the wine bottles.

Take the box and use sandpaper to remove any residual chemical agent.

If you don't have the box, try to build it with wooden planks: take a square or rectangular one for the bottom, two long and narrow ones for the sides and two more to attach obliquely for the roof and fix them with nails and wood screws.

Measure the depth of the box and cut the bamboo rods accordingly so that they can be inserted inside.

Place the rods next to each other: from the outside the hole must be easily accessible. Glue the rods together with hot glue, filling up to about half or 2/3 of the height of the box.

Now take the lid of the box and draw with a pencil the shape of a small door, to be applied on the space not filled with the rods: cut it with the jigsaw to size, then drill it regularly, with holes of different sizes and horizontal and vertical slots, in order to attract different species of useful insects. Fix the door with a zipper to open it and fill the space with sticks and straw.

You can attach the insect shed to the outside wall of a building (house, box, shed), at a height of about 1.50 metres (calculated from the lower edge of the shed), preferably sheltered from the rain. You can also choose a tree if possible: avoid light sources instead. It seems obvious to say so but know that, to do its job, the shed must be close to the rest of the vegetation.

Fasten the house firmly to the wall or tree: with pressure anchors, with wood screws in case of use on wooden supports and with webbing and tie-rods in case of fixing to a tree (you will avoid damaging it).

Expose the house to east-south/east-south-west. If after one year the insects have not settled in the house you have prepared, change exposure and position.

To make it easier for insects to enter the house at the end of winter, you can leave it all year round.

Do not paint the shed with conventional paints, but treat it with non-toxic products and water-based paints. Do not mount it on metal surfaces.

A "bug-caller" garden

Now that you've built your little house, how do you make sure it attracts useful insects? It is not necessarily enough to place it in the garden for them to "inhabit" it! Some tricks can be used to attract insects called "entomophagi", which are "good" insects that feed on other "bad" insects, avoiding the use of harmful insecticides.

To attract useful insects such as ladybugs and apoids, you can sow colourful plants and flowers in pots or gardens: for example, marigold, potted marigold, dandelion, cornflower and fragrant pea. Ladybugs also love "fragrant" vegetables such as horseradish, cauliflower and broccoli.

For hoverflies, bees and wasps, pollinators par excellence, plant echinacea and geraniums.

Carrots, fennel and alyssum (perennial herbaceous plants of the Brassicaceae family) provide the nectar needed to feed many "good" insects such as hoverflies (small insects that imitate bees and wasps in colour: the larvae feed on aphids, adults are excellent pollinators).

Aromatic plants are also able to attract useful insects or to ward off parasites: nettle, useful against aphids; garlic, a well-known natural pesticide; sage, which attracts bees in particular; thyme, appreciated by hoverflies and coriander.

CHAPTER 14 - Hydroponics Plantation

The term Hydroponics was re-invented in the mid-twentieth century. The concept of plants growing without soil dates back to prehistoric times. The mythical hanging gardens of Babylon, the floods of the Nile and the floating gardens of Mexico City are all examples of hydroponic systems. History, as always, has transformed the circle and the age of hydroponics has returned to our times.

Why use this type of cultivation?

1. Nutrition - abundant, no deficiencies or toxicity. You can have total control over the administration of hydroponic fertilizers.
2. Yield - 2 to 10 times more than growing in soil! Super speed in growth with an abundant final yield.
3. Water - saving 80%. You don't have to water every day; it is the same water that is used and recirculated by an irrigation system.
4. Diseases - no soil viruses or bacteria. In the absence of soil and organic matter there are almost no diseases.
5. Weeds - practically none. Inability of weeds to grow in the hydroponic system.
6. Quality - higher, better, healthier. Thanks to the absolute control of the values the plant grows in the best way increasing the quality and the final taste.
7. Maturity - you can choose, it is not seasonal, faster! Possibility to grow in continuous cycles 12 months out of 12.

How hydroponic cultivation works

The plants are grown in a sterile inert growth medium, such as rockwool, clay, perlite, vermiculite and fed with a mixture of water and nutrients. The principle is fundamental, plants that are grown in soils must continuously develop their root system in search of water and nutrients so most of the plant's energy is used for root development and limits its superior growth. Consider that water, nutrients and air is supplied directly to the plant, freeing it from unnecessary energy expenditure and giving it a balance between root and stem. By giving all the nutrients, air and water you could want, your plants grow much faster and with an optimal yield equivalent to 100%.

The key to your success for optimal hydroponic growing is light, air and nutrient solution. The nutrient solution is, in other words, water with nutrients. It must contain all the mineral elements necessary for plant growth and must be in the right proportions. Nothing can be left to chance. Fortunately, there is a wide range of hydroponic fertilizers available and it is simply a matter of choosing the product that best suits your needs.

Useful tips for success in hydroponics

For a good start, it is imperative that quality water is inserted into the system tank. The tap water must be checked with an EC and TDS meter. If the value exceeds 150ppm a reverse osmosis filter should be used.

In addition, the amount of oxygen in the water is very important for plants and we recommend using an oxygen pump.

Another tip is to give the plants, in addition to the classic N-P-K fertilizers, boosters rich in vitamins and microelements that can enrich the life cycle of the plants themselves. For the flowering phase, in addition to the classic fertilisers, you can also use a booster that can double the flowers or fruits of your plants, the BioBizz Top Max.

Remember that the pH and ec of the solution should be measured daily and the solution should be replaced once every 2 weeks. Also remember that the pH of the solution tends to increase with nutrient administration, so it is recommended to measure the pH after adding fertilizer to the solution.

Usually before harvesting hydroponics growers tend to purify the plants. This can be done by replacing the nutrient solution with simple water for the last 7 /10 days. This technique called "flashing" allows you to remove any fertilizer in the plant tissue and improves the taste and aroma of the final product.

CONCLUSIONS

In conclusion, we hope that "Companion Planting for Beginners" has been a helpful and informative guide for you on your journey to growing your own organic produce. We thank you for taking the time to read this book and trust that you have gained valuable knowledge and insights into companion planting. Our goal is that you will be able to successfully implement what you have learned and reach your gardening goals. We wish you the best of luck and hope that you will enjoy the fruits (literally) of your labor!

www.ingramcontent.com/pod-product-compliance
Lightning Source LLC
Chambersburg PA
CBHW050240120526
44590CB00016B/2164